Dark psychology secrets

Dark psychology and manipulation guide for beginners. Mastery of mind control and learning how to influence people

[Dale Eckhart]

Table of Contents

Introduction

Dark Psychology is the art of manipulation and the control of one's mind. Personality scholars agree that there is a personality profile, the dark triad, that determines certain behaviors socially or extremely selfish that involve suffering from others and skip social norms, thinking only of their benefits over anything or person.

Dark psychology is going to be any type of deviant or criminal behaviors that are committed against others, usually innocent victims. The one using dark psychology is going to prey on someone who they see as weaker or vulnerable. This doesn't mean they are actually weak, but they can be easily influenced or easily read for the benefit of the manipulator.

Dark psychology is always present in the world. There are always those who will search for the weaknesses in others, in order to benefit themselves. They will use lying, withholding of love, persuasion, and manipulation in order to get what they want. And they are often successful at it because they can easily read the person they are trying to target.

Many people live in denial. They assume that dark psychology is not there and that it is not really a problem they need to deal with. But thinking that this type of psychology isn't even there is a bad choice. You can choose to remain ignorant of this, or you can learn how to take control so that you can protect yourself and others from those who would like to cause you harm or ruin you.

Being able to understand dark psychology is not just a defensive measure. There are a lot of principles and ideas found within the world of dark psychology. And simply by knowing them, you will be able to be on the lookout for someone using these techniques. This kind of knowledge is going to be useful whenever someone tries to use those techniques against you.

Once you have pulled back the curtain of the world of dark psychology, you will find that there is so much more to human nature than you ever imagined. Let's take a look at how this can work.

The dark triad (or the Dark triad) is a personality profile based on a combination of the following three factors:

Psychopathy (Psychopathy): is a person with a tough personality, "callous," cruelty behaviors, and a very limited empathy. They are people who have no remorse, moral, or ethical standards are indifferent, and are often cynical and insensitive.

Machiavellianism (Machiavellianism): people with superficial charm and very manipulative. For example, they are people who can use other people to get what they want; they lie, they take advantage of who they can cheat and cheat.

Narcissism (Narcissism) consists of belief of superiority, grandiosity and vanity, and high emotional explosiveness. They are people who want everyone to admire them and pay attention to them, who believe they deserve a higher status or a social prestige and who expect special and favorable treatment and who, if they are not treated as they think they deserve, can react with anger, rage or aggressiveness.

Also, they are usually people with an unpleasant treatment (even being superficially charming), with very limited self-control (they can be very nice and suddenly have a fit of anger), they are usually aggressive, not very responsible and are not honest.

There is a great difference between the sexes, because it is much more frequent to find this personality profile in men than in women, unlike other personality profiles (such as an anxious profile).

What is manipulative behavior?

Deception is central to manipulative behavior. Very manipulative people are experts in the game of deception and in combination with the general coldness that they (often) have, they are merciless.

People who manipulate a lot often do not see people as living beings, but rather as a means to reach a goal.

That often means that once they have arrived at their 'destination,' they will certainly not think twice about leaving you on the side of the road.

The worst part is that they sometimes want to play it so that you are the guilty one and they are the victim. That is the tricky thing with people with manipulative behavior.

From small things about insisting that you come to their office or take you by surprise and immediately make a choice that is also part of the manipulation. This is also in line with one of the other important parts of manipulative behavior: intimidation.

Manipulators like to intimidate and belittle because it puts them in their position of power and puts them above others.

People also manipulate for power and money, but also status and vanity. So manipulation is often the improvement of one's situation (at the expense of others!)

Causes of manipulative behavior

Unfortunately, the cliché that people who show manipulative behavior during their youth have been mistreated or have suffered trauma is true.

Being physically abused by parents or emotionally by, for example, narcissistic parents can have a huge effect on a child who can express himself in terribly nasty ways.

Another reason that people behave manipulatively is when there is a lot at stake, such as in politics.

A certain type of people will do everything to stay in power once they have experienced it, with all the consequences that entail.

Many narcissistic people, such as managers and politicians, do everything to maintain their power and status.

This is often also why a 'ladder' is created at schools and universities with a group of people who will do everything to stay 'at the top.'

The parties, luxury houses and cars, expensive watches, and designer clothing, everything is about them to convey a sense of authority. Often these people are also narcissists.

However, there are also people who naturally have the impulse to behave manipulatively, and they are often found in the situations mentioned above. These people are also called psychopaths.

Examples of manipulative behavior

Although this may all sound a bit far away and perhaps even unrealistic, manipulative behavior is more than enough in everyday life:

You wrote an important file yesterday afternoon and gave it to a colleague so that they could look at it again and then send it.

When you came to work this morning, your boss was at your desk and started screaming angrily that you never wrote that file.

So after the boss was finished, you went on high legs to your colleague, and something very strange happened: your colleague claimed that you never gave him that file, but he did it in such a convincing way that you started your memory to doubt!

This is gas lighting and is a textbook example of manipulative behavior.

Manipulative people will also not accept guilt under any circumstances:

You and a friend fought this week, and after thinking about it for a while, you also concluded that you might have reacted a bit exaggerated.

You determine to go to your friend's house to make it up, and after you apologize and get accepted, you notice that your friend did not apologize.

If you ask for it subtly, the answer is short: "No, of course, I don't have to apologize! If you hadn't done that stupid, I wouldn't have gotten angry. "

This is, of course, strange reasoning and is almost iconic for manipulative behavior.

There is one good example of manipulative behavior:

You were ill this week, and that is why you were sick at home all week. It was so bad that even walking from the bed to the couch was too much trouble.

Fortunately, one week later you feel a little better, and if you are down the line later that week to encourage your son to play football, you tell one of the parents along the line about it who took your son last week because was sick.

The answer was not what you expected:

"Is that all? That's nothing, man! Last year I was so sick that I bruised my lungs, I coughed so hard! And yet I stood along the line! Because you should be there for your children, you just don't have to put yourself up like that and just come along. You are a good parent, aren't you? "

Not only was this a bad answer (because you were sick last week and you really couldn't), it was also a manipulative answer.

The parent has not only minimized your problems and put them in the spotlight, but they have also belittled you.

Chapter 1: What is dark psychology

Before we take a look at some of the methods that come with dark psychology and how it can be used against you, it is important to know exactly what this form of psychology is about. Psychology, or an understanding of how the human mind works, is a part of all of our lives. Psychology is going to underpin everything in our lives from advertising to finance, crime to religion, and even from hate to love. Someone who is able to understand these psychological principles is someone who really holds onto the key to human influence.

This is not an easy task, which is why most people don't possess it. Learning all of the different principles of psychology is not necessary. Start with the lessons in these pages and you'll have a solid foundation. You have to be able to read people, understand what makes them tick, and understand why they may react in ways that may not be normally expected. And even then, you may need to spend time taking classes and reading through countless books to gain a complete understanding. It depends how far you want to go with this.

So, if only a few people really understand psychology and how the human mind works, why is it so important to know what this is? It is because those who do know what it is and how to use it can choose to use that power and that knowledge against you.

How Is Dark Psychology Used Today?

While some people are going to use these dark psychology tactics in order to harm their victim, there are times when you may use these tactics without the intent of negatively manipulating another person. Some of these tactics were either unintentionally or intentionally added to our toolbox from a variety of means that could include:

- When you were a child, you would see how adults, especially those close to you, behaved.

- When you were a teenager, the mind and your ability to truly understand the behaviors around you were expanded.

- You were able to watch others use the tactics and then succeed.

- Using the tactics may have been unintentional in the beginning, but when you found that it worked to get you what you wanted, you would start to use those tactics in an intentional manner.

- Some people, such as a politician, a public speaker, or a salesperson, would be trained to use these types of tactics to get what they want.

Dark Psychology Tactics That Are Used on a Regular Basis

- Love flooding: This would include any buttering up, praising, or complimenting people to get them to comply with the request that you want. If you want someone to help you move some items into your home, you may use love flooding in order to make them feel good, which could make it more likely that they will help you. A dark manipulator could also use it to make the other person feel attached to them and then get them to do things that they may not normally do.

- Lying: This would include telling the victim an untrue version of the situation. It can also include a partial truth or exaggerations with the goal of getting what you wanted done.

- Love denial: This one can be hard on the victim because it can make them feel lost and abandoned by the manipulator. This one basically includes withholding affection and love until you are able to get what you want out of the victim.

- Withdrawal: This would be when the victim is given the silent treatment or is avoided until they meet the needs of the other person.

- Restricting choices: The manipulator may give their victim access to some choices, but they do this in order to distract them from the choices that they don't want the victim to make.

- Semantic manipulation: This is a technique where the manipulator is going to use some commonly known words, ones that have accepted meanings by both parties, in a conversation. But then they will tell the victim, later on, that they had meant something completely different when they used that word. The new meaning is often going to change up the entire definition and could make it so that the conversation goes the way the manipulator wanted, even though the victim was tricked.

- Reverse psychology: This is when you tell someone to do something in one manner, knowing that they will do the opposite. But the opposite action is what the manipulator wanted to happen in the first place.

Who Will Deliberately Use Dark Tactics?

There are many different people who may choose to use these dark tactics against you. They can be found in many different aspects of your life, which is why it is so important to learn how to stay away from them. Some of the people who are able to use some of these dark psychology tactics deliberately include:

- Narcissists: These individuals are going to have a bloated sense of their own self-worth, and they will have the need to make others believe that they are superior as well. In order to meet their desires of being worshipped and adored by everyone they meet, they will use persuasion and dark psychology.

- Sociopaths: Those who are sociopaths are charming, intelligent, and persuasive. But they only act this way to get what they want. They lack any emotions and they are not able to feel any remorse. This means that they have no issue with using the tactics of dark psychology to get what they want, including taking it as far as creating superficial relationships.

- Politicians: With the help of dark psychology, a politician could convince someone to cast votes for them simply by convincing these people that their point of view is the right one.

- Salespeople: Not all salespeople are going to use dark tactics against you. But it is possible that some, especially those who are really into getting their sales numbers and being the best, will not think twice about using dark persuasion in order to manipulate people.

- Leaders: Throughout history, there have been plenty of leaders who will use the techniques of dark psychology in order to get their team members, subordinates, and citizens do what they want.

- Selfish people: This could be any person that you come across who will make sure that their own needs are put before anyone else's. They aren't concerned about others, and they will let others forego their benefits so that they can benefit. If the situation benefits them, it is fine if it benefits someone else. But if someone is going to be the loser, it will be the other person and not them.

This list is important because it is going to serve two purposes. First, it is going to help you be more aware of the people who may try to manipulate you to do things that you don't want to do, and it can be there to help out with self-realization. Being on the lookout for those who want to get something out of you, without any concerns about how it will affect you, is one of the main goals of this book so that you can arm yourself against dark psychology.

Chapter 2: Techniques used for dark persuasion

Persuasion is an interesting topic. There are lots of persuasions that are considered just fine in society. They are acceptable and even some people hold jobs where they will spend a lot of time trying to persuade others. Any attempt by one person to influence someone else to do some action can be persuasion. A salesperson at a car dealership is using persuasion because they try to persuade someone to purchase a new vehicle. This isn't seen as something sinister or bad. The difference here is that this persuasion and other similar examples of persuasion benefit both parties. The car dealer makes a sale and some money, and the "victim" is going to get a new vehicle.

There are a lot of legitimate types of persuasion that aren't considered part of dark psychology. The car dealer above is an example. If a negotiator uses their skills to persuade a terrorist to let their hostage go, this is a good form of persuasion. If you convince someone to come along to an event that they will enjoy, then this is a good form of persuasion. This type of persuasion is seen as positive persuasion. But then, what would count as dark persuasion?

Understanding Dark Persuasion

The first difference you will notice between positive and dark persuasion is the motive behind it. Positive persuasion is used in order to encourage someone to complete an action that isn't going to cause them any harm. In some cases, such as with the negotiator saving a hostage, this persuasion can be used to help save lives.

If positive persuasion is understood as a way to help people help themselves, then dark persuasion is more of the process of making people act against their own self-interest. Sometimes, people are going to do these actions begrudgingly, knowing that they are probably not making the right choice, but they do it because they are eager to stop the incessant persuasion efforts. In other cases, the best dark persuader is going to make their victim think that they acted wisely, but the victim is actually doing the opposite in that case.

So, what are the motivations for someone who is a dark persuader? This is going to depend on the situation and the individual who is doing the persuading. Some people like to persuade their victims in order to serve their own self-interests. Others are going to act through with the intention just to cause some harm to the other person. In some cases, the persuader is not going to really benefit from darkly persuading their victim, but they do so because they want to inflict pain on the other person. And still, others enjoy the control that this kind of persuasion gives to them.

Persuasion techniques can frequently go under various other names as well as be described in such means as persuasion techniques as well as persuasion techniques. There is not simply one technique that can be utilized to convince somebody to assume or act in a specific means. The representative might have the ability to speak to the topic while offering proof in order to change the topic's mind, they might have the ability to utilize some kind of pressure or draw they have versus the topic, and also they can carry out some type of solution for the topic, or make use of an additional strategy. This area will certainly enter into even more information concerning the various techniques of persuasion that are readily available as well as just how each of them could be reliable in the procedure of persuasion.

Use of Pressure

Depending upon the circumstance, the representative might determine it is an excellent concept to utilize some pressure in order to encourage the based on believe their means. This might occur if the suggestions do not pair up properly, normal talking is not functioning, or when the representative is coming to be aggravated or distressed with the turn of the discussion. Commonly pressure is utilized as a kind of scare technique since it offers the subject much less time to assume practically regarding what is taking place contrasted to when a typical discussion happens. Generally pressure will certainly be made use of when the representative has actually had much less success making use of the various other ways of persuasion that are readily available, although beginning with making use of pressure is in some cases done too. At various other times, pressure might be made use of if the representative seems like they are blowing up or when the topic has the ability to existing inconsistent proof to the representative and also the representative blows up.

Frequently it is not the most effective concept to utilize pressure when it concerns the procedure of persuasion. This is because lots of topics will certainly see making use of pressure as a risk because of the reality that the representative will certainly not provide various other choices to the demand that they are making. The entire allure of persuasion is that it provides the subject the selection of courses, once pressure is brought right into the mix, that liberty of option is gone as well as the topic is more probable to really feel endangered. When the subject really feels endangered, they are much less most likely to pay attention as well as take into consideration anything that the representative is claiming therefore the procedure will certainly not go any kind of additionally. Because of these factors, using pressure is normally prevented and also prevented in the art of persuasion; unlike the various other types of mind control gone over.

Reciprocity

The initial tool of impact is the concept of reciprocity. This concept specifies that when a single person, the representative, gives the various other individual, the topic, with something of worth, the topic is mosting likely to try to pay back the representative in kind. This essentially indicates, when the representative carries out some sort of solution to the topic, the topic will certainly really feel that they have a responsibility to do a comparable solution to the representative at a long time. While both solutions could not equal, they have the very same type of worth to make sure that the commitment of each is equated to out.

The act of reciprocation winds up generating a feeling of commitment in the topic, which the representative will certainly after that have the ability to make use of as an effective device when they intend to utilize persuasion. The guideline of reciprocity is extremely efficient due to the fact that it aids the representative obtain the topic right into the right mindset for the act of persuasion by instilling as well as subduing the topic with a feeling of responsibility. The representative might be most likely to obtain the subject persuaded to do or act a specific method since the topic will certainly have that feeling of commitment dangling over them.

An additional included advantage for the representative being used reciprocity is that it is not simply an ethical standing that will certainly place the responsibility on the topic; it is likewise a standing that is stood up by social codes. The representative is not mosting likely to require to stress over whether the topic has the best values to return the support. If the topic does not really feel the requirement to do so, the representative has some devices offered to stimulate them right into activity.

As a culture, individuals do not such as people that are irresponsible in returning a support or repayment when they are used a cost-free present or solution. If the representative does not really feel like the topic is mosting likely to reciprocate to them, they will certainly have the ability to transform them in to their social team. They can do this by informing various other pals or colleagues regarding just how they did a support for the subject however the subject never ever returned it when it was required. Currently the representative has actually compelled social criteria on the topic via the informing of the support, making it much more most likely that they will certainly have the ability to encourage the topic right into doing something.

Generally, the topic will certainly enjoy to reciprocate to the representative without requiring any kind of outdoors pressures. When the support is approved, the topic will certainly start to seek manner ins which they can settle the representative to make sure that ball game is also as well as they do not appear money grubbing or self-seeking. The representative will certainly after that have the ability to offer a simple remedy to the topic on exactly how to settle this financial obligation; the topic will certainly really feel appreciation at having this very easy service as well as will certainly be more probable to go the manner in which the representative desires.

Dedication and also Uniformity

The following tool of impact that is to be reviewed is that of dedication and also uniformity. The representative is mosting likely to require to make use of both of these if they want to encourage any person to alter to their viewpoint. When points correspond, they are simpler to recognize as well as can assist the based on make their choices much better. It does refrain well for the representative to constantly transform the realities that they are making use of or to transform various other info that is required in order to assist the subject procedure the info. As opposed to assisting with the procedure of encouraging, continuously avoiding uniformity is mosting likely to make the representative appear like a phony as well as somebody that can not be relied on, causing the failing of the persuasion procedure.

Uniformity is among one of the most vital facets of the persuasion procedure. This is due to the fact that:

- Uniformity is valued very in culture: individuals like to have points remain a specific method the majority of the moment. While there is a great deal of selection in every day life, individuals really feel secure understanding that total points will certainly remain quite constant. It enables them to bear in mind what has actually taken place, recognize what to anticipate, and also be prepared if any type of modifications do take place to take place. If uniformity were not offered, points would certainly be extremely hard to strategy as well as there would certainly constantly be problems of mayhem walking around. If you desire to convince a topic of a specific point, after that you need to see to it that your realities correspond and also make good sense to them.

- Uniformity causes profiting the every day life technique of most individuals. Have you ever before attempted to intend a day out when something unforeseen turns up? It can make points practically difficult to do as well as will certainly wind up sensation like a calamity. Individuals like uniformity since it enables them to recognize what to anticipate and also what to do. They recognize when it is time to consume, when it is time for job, and also when various other points will certainly take place throughout the day.

- Uniformity supplies a faster way that is extremely beneficial via the difficulties existing in contemporary presence. Life is challenging sufficient without needing to include various other points that do not make given that. When individuals have the ability to have regular lives, it makes points a great deal much easier.

- Uniformity is a wonderful device due to the fact that it permits the subject the capability to make the right choices as well as to refine details. If the representative wishes to achieve success in their ventures of convincing the topic, they require to see to it that their message corresponds. There is no space for incorrect proof that can turn up later on as well as destroy the entire procedure. Maintain the truths honest as well as succinct as well as it is far better for encouraging the topic.

Something that connects uniformity is the act of dedication. In order to recognize that the topic is in fact encouraged which the initiative has actually repaid, it is essential to have some sort of dedication in position. In advertising and marketing, this can indicate that the topic is mosting likely to buy the item or in national politics it can suggest that the topic will certainly elect a specific prospect. The dedication that is made will certainly differ relying on the nature of the persuasion. According to the idea of uniformity, if an individual devotes, either in composing or by mouth, they are a lot more most likely to recognize the dedication that they have actually made.

It has actually been discovered that this is a lot more real in regards to created dedications considering that the topic will certainly be extra concrete emotionally as well as there is some tough evidence that they consented to the dedication. This makes a great deal of feeling; lots of people will certainly assure by mouth that they will certainly repair something or do something, simply to reverse as well as refrain it. Certain, some individuals will certainly do what they claimed, as well as they are most likely to do it if encouraging by mouth than not assuring in all, yet usually it is still tough to obtain the outcomes that you desire by doing this. On top of that, there is no other way to back it up considering that a dental arrangement will certainly simply come to be a he claimed she stated argument as well as nobody will certainly win. On the various other hand, if the representative has the ability to create a created dedication from the topic, they have the evidence they require that things has actually been done.

The factor that it is so essential for the representative to obtain the based on consent to a dedication is since when the topic has actually dedicated to the brand-new position, they have even more of a propensity to act in a manner that is suitable to that dedication. Afterwards factor, the topic will certainly advance as well as start to take part in self-persuasion for the reason. They will certainly give themselves together with others with different reasons and also factors to sustain the dedication to avoid any type of problems with the representative. If the representative has the ability to obtain the based on that factor, the representative will certainly have a whole lot much less job to take care of.

<u>**Social Evidence**</u>

Persuasion is a kind of social communication as well as a result is mosting likely to require to adhere to the social regulations where it is taking place. The topic is mosting likely to be affected by the individuals that are around them; they are mosting likely to be more probable to wish to do what others are doing instead of do their very own point. The topic will certainly base their ideas and also activity according to what others are doing around them, exactly how these very same individuals act, and also just how they think. As an example, if the subject matures in a city, they are most likely to imitate others that are from that location; on the various other hand, those that mature in an area that is extremely spiritual might invest a great deal of their time hoping, discovering, as well as assisting others.

Under this idea the claiming "the power of the group," can be extremely reliable. The topic is mosting likely to wish to know what other individuals around them are doing in any way times. It has actually come to be nearly a fixation in this nation to be able to do what others are carrying out in order to suit, although that individuals will certainly claim exactly how they wish to be various and also be a person.

We spent some time in the last chapter exploring what dark seduction is about and why someone may choose to use this kind of seduction to get what they want out of a relationship. And now that we know a bit more about the guiding principles that come behind these approaches to seduction, it is time to learn some of the techniques that the dark seducer can use to make dark seduction work for them.

The first approach that we will look at is known as the indirect approach. One mistake that you may see in conventional dating is that one or both parties will offer an icebreaker, one that is usually unappealing and cheesy, when they try to introduce themselves to someone new. They may say something like "You look pretty," "Nice eyes," or "Good song, right?"

Why are these icebreakers so bad? It is likely that the victim of your seduction has heard these countless times, and as soon as they hear them, they will be turned off and not want to talk to you at all. When the seducer uses such a bad line, it often leaves the impression that they are unappealing and bland, and no one wants to waste their time on a relationship with that kind of person.

With the indirect opener, the seducer is throwing in a breath of fresh air compared to the opening lines we talked about before. An indirect opener is going to be an icebreaker that will start the social interaction but won't convey any sexual intent. Often it is going to be posed as an "intriguing question." A good example of this would be when the seducer asks something like "Settle this for me or my buddies over there – do men or women lie more?" This is a different way to open up and talk with the other person and can start up a new conversation. And it shows the victim that the seducer is very interesting and is interested in a good conversation.

An instance that is provided concerning just how individuals will certainly do something since others are doing it can be located with a phone-a-thon. If the host claims something like "Operators are waiting, please phone call currently," the topic might seem like there are drivers that are relaxing with absolutely nothing to do since no person is calling them. This will certainly make the subject much less most likely to call since they figure if another person isn't calling after that they should not either. If the host simply alters a couple of words as well as rather claims "If drivers are hectic, please telephone call once again," there can be an extremely various outcome. The topic is currently mosting likely to presume that the drivers are active with the telephone calls of numerous others topics so the company have to be excellent as well as legit. The topic will certainly be far more most likely to contact whether they survive today or need to be postponed.

The persuasion strategy of social evidence is one of the most reliable in circumstances where the topic doubts of what they will certainly do or when there appear to be lots of resemblances in the scenarios. In uncertain or unsure scenarios that have several options or opportunities to be made, the topic will certainly usually select to adapt what others around them are doing. This is since the options are so comparable that any one of them will certainly function, however they will certainly presume that the selection the others are making is the one that is right. The various other manner in which social evidence can be made use of is when there are some resemblances taking place. For instance, the topic is a lot more most likely to adapt as well as alter around those that resemble them somehow. If there is somebody that resembles the topic that supervises, the topic is most likely to pay attention as well as follow them greater than if the boss is really various from the topic.

The representative will certainly have the ability to utilize the suggestion of social evidence to aid with their procedure of persuasion. The very first means they can do this is seeing the phrasing that they are stating. With the instance offered of the video game program, both of the quotes were stating the very same point, yet by changing up the phrasing they created 2 various significances. Neither of them were a lie; they were simply efficient at generating a various type of feedback. If the representative has the ability to view the manner in which they word points, they can generate the ideal feedback out of their topics as well as encourage the based on comply with the exact same concepts as well as ideas.

On top of that, the representative will certainly discover that there is even more success if they have the ability to obtain those that resemble them to cooperate the suggestions. This is why political leaders will certainly attempt to project to teams with the comparable concepts to them. If they require to get to a bigger team, they will certainly customize their concepts in order to make them extra attractive to these brand-new teams.

Taste

The representative is mosting likely to function really hard so as to get the based on like them. There is an extremely basic factor or this;

if the subject suches as the representative, they are a lot more most likely to claim yes to them. There are 2 primary elements that will certainly add to just how well the subject suches as the representative. The very first one is physical good looks as well as the 2nd is resemblance.

For the initial one, if the representative is much more appealing literally to the topic, they are mosting likely to have the sensation of being a lot more convincing given that they have the ability to obtain what they desire a lot more quickly while additionally altering the mindsets of others. This beauty variable has actually been verified reliable in sending out beneficial messages and also perceptions of various other qualities that the representative might have consisting of knowledge, compassion, and also skill. This all interact to make it most likely that an appealing individual will certainly have the ability to extra conveniently convince the topic.

The 2nd variable, resemblance, is a little less complex. The concept specifies that if the topic resembles the representative, they are a lot more most likely to address in the affirmative to what the representative is asking. This procedure is quite all-natural and also the majority of the moment the topic will certainly not need to consider whether it is the ideal point to do when they such as and also resemble the representative.

<u>**Authority**</u>

Among the manner in which the representative will certainly achieve success in encouraging the topic is to come to be an authority. There is a propensity in the majority of people to think that something a professional claims on a topic holds true. The topic is most likely to delight in paying attention to a representative that is credible and also well-informed; this suggests that if the representative can bring these 2 points to the table, after that they are currently heading to obtaining their based on pay attention and also think them.

There have actually been researches done to demonstrate how this authority strategy can operate in convincing the based on pay attention to what the representative needs to claim. The research study done was referred to as the Milgram research study as well as was really an entire collection of experiments began in 1961. The individuals included 2 topics and also each was put right into various spaces. The initial topic was after that affixed to a harness that was electrical and also which might carry out the shock. The 2nd topic was advised by the representative, that was spruced up in a researcher's layer as well as looked authorities, to ask the very first subject inquiries and afterwards to penalize them whenever a concern was addressed inaccurately. The 2nd topic was asked by the representative to supply electric shocks that originated from a panel that was under the 2nd topic's control. After supplying a shock, the 2nd topic needed to choose the following greatest voltage to make use of the following time as well as would certainly remain to do this till the greatest voltage of 450 volts was gotten to.

One point that was not recognized to the 2nd topic was that the very first topic was just a star that was forging the discomfort; this very first topic was not in fact being damaged while doing so. This experiment was performed in order to see exactly how well the 2nd topic would certainly comply with a person responsible, not to hurt somebody deliberately. The declaration that supported this research study was "When an authority informs average individuals it is their task to supply damage, just how much suffering will each subject agree to bring upon on a totally innocent individual if the guidelines originate from over?" According to this research, the majority of the 2nd topics agreed to give as much discomfort to the very first topic as was offered. This caused the final thought that a lot of topics agree to put discomfort upon others if they are informed to do so by an authority number of some type.

Certainly, when it pertains to persuasion, discomfort is not something that is needed in any way times in order to alter the manner in which individuals assume. This research study was simply a picture of just how the topic is mosting likely to respond to the representative if the representative has the ability to show they are some type of tyrannical individual. Maintaining this in mind can assist the representative to reach their very own schedule.

<u>Shortage</u>

Shortage is an additional kind of persuasion that individuals might know with yet which is frequently undervalued. When an item or suggestion has a minimal accessibility, it is most likely to be appointed a greater worth. According to Cialdini "individuals desire even more of what they can not have." While this could seem like it is defining a kid that is attempting to get involved in the cookie container when they are informed no, it can likewise define exactly how routine grownups will certainly act. When there is the concern of shortage to take into consideration, the context is mosting likely to matter too. This merely indicates that within particular contexts, the suggestion of deficiency could in fact be a benefit.

The representative of persuasion will certainly have the ability to make use of the concept of shortage to their benefit. They will certainly require to discover a method to make the subject think that the thing is limited by clarifying why that thing is so unique and also what it does that absolutely nothing else has the ability to do. The representative is mosting likely to need to function their topic in properly. The representative can additionally select to go the various other method; as opposed to describing what the consumer will certainly acquire by the product or suggestion, they can clarify what they will certainly shed by not having the thing. For instance, the representative can claim something like "you will certainly shed $5" instead of opting for "you can conserve $5". This is simply an additional manner in which the representative will certainly have the ability to make something seem like it is scarcer.

There are 2 reasons that this concept of deficiency jobs. First of all, when things or items are challenging to get, they will typically get even more worth. The even more worth a product has the far better high quality it will certainly appear to have, also if this is not real.

If something is simple to obtain, nobody will certainly desire it as long as when the product is harder. If the representative has the ability to grow the concept that their ideas, ideas, or products are limited as well as challenging to find by, they will certainly have a much greater possibility of seeing success in their persuasion initiatives.

Persuasion Methods

The strategies that feature persuasion have actually been observed as well as examined for several years, completely back to old times. This has actually been done since impact is so beneficial to a wide range of various individuals. The official research of these strategies has actually expanded beginning in the very early 20th century. Considering that the utmost objective of making use of persuasion is to encourage the based on take the convincing disagreement, internalize it, and afterwards embrace it as a brand-new mindset, there is a great deal of worth in finding which methods of persuasion are one of the most effective. The 3 persuasion strategies that supply one of the most worth to the representative as well as which will certainly be talked about in this area are developing a demand, attracting the social requirements, as well as making use of packed pictures and also words.

Produce a Demand

One manner in which the representative is mosting likely to have the ability to obtain the conditional their mind-set is to produce a requirement or they can interest a demand that currently existed in the topic. This kind of persuasion will certainly interest the subject if done properly; this indicates that for the representative to be effective they will certainly require to attract the basic requirements of the subject such as their requirement for self-actualization, self-confidence, love, food, and also sanctuary. The factor that this technique is mosting likely to function so well for the representative is since the topic is really mosting likely to require these points. Food is not something that they will certainly have the ability to make it through without for long. If the representative has the ability to convince the topic that their shop is the very best or by changing their ideas they would certainly have the ability to obtain even more food or sanctuary, there is a greater opportunity for success.

Interesting Social Requirements

Next off, the representative might interest the social demands of the topic. While social demands are not as reliable to utilize as the key requirements, they are still a vital device that can be utilized. Individuals like to be desired and also component of the group. They such as the reputation that some things have the ability to provide and also to seem like they belong in a greater social standing. The concept of attracting the social demands of the topic can be located in a lot of tv commercials that get on; in these commercials the audience will certainly be urged to purchase a product to make sure that they can end up being popular or be much like every person else. When the representative interest the social requirements of the topic, they have the ability to get to a brand-new location that could fascinate the topic.

Making Use Of Packed Photos and also Words

When it involves persuasion, the selection of words that are made can make every one of the distinction. There are several means to state the very same point yet one means could stimulate the topic right into activity while the various other will certainly not. Claiming the appropriate words the proper way is mosting likely to make every one of the distinction when it pertains to making use of persuasion. The instance regarding the phone-a-thon previously in this phase is a fine example of exactly how words can be utilized to encourage based on delve into activity.

Persuasion is an effective device of mind control that is frequently taken too lightly and also neglected. Possibly this is due to the fact that it supplies even more of a selection to the subject contrasted to the various other types of mind control. In the various other choices, the topic is pushed into entry, occasionally alone, by the representative and also winds up not having a lot of a selection in what is taking place while doing so. In regards to persuasion, the truths exist to ensure that the topic has the ability to compose their very own mind, also if the truths are positioned in a particular method to reveal them in the most effective light.

Chapter 3: Brainwashing

Brainwashing is the main sort of mind control to talk about. Mentally conditioning is fundamentally the procedure where somebody will be schemed to forsake convictions that they had in the past so as to make new goals and qualities. There is a lot of ways this should be possible in spite of the fact that not every one of them will be viewed as terrible.

For instance, on the off chance that you are from an African nation and, at that point move to America, you will frequently be compelled to change your qualities and goals so as to fit in with the new culture and surroundings that you are in. Then again, those in inhumane imprisonments or when another despot government is assuming control over, they will regularly experience the way toward mentally programming so as to persuade residents to track with calmly. Numerous individuals have confusions of what mentally conditioning is.

A few people have increasingly suspicious thoughts regarding the work on including mind control gadgets that are supported by the administration and that are believed to be effectively turned on like a remote control. On the opposite side of things, there are doubters who don't accept that mentally programming is conceivable at all and that any individual who cases it has happened is lying.

Generally, the act of mental programming will arrive at some place amidst these two thoughts. During the act of mentally conditioning, the subject will be persuaded to change their convictions about something through a blend of various strategies. There isn't only one methodology that can be utilized during this procedure so it very well may be hard to put the training into a perfect little box.

Generally, the subject will be isolated from everything that they know. From that point, they will be separated into an enthusiastic express that makes them powerless before the new ideas are presented. As the subject ingests this new data, they will be compensated for communicating thoughts and contemplations which oblige these new thoughts.

The compensating is the thing that will be utilized so as to fortify the mental programming that is happening. Mentally conditioning isn't something that is new to the society. Individuals have been utilizing these systems for quite a while. For instance, in an authentic setting, the individuals who were detainees of wars were regularly separated before being influenced to changes sides.

The absolute best instances of these would result in the detainee turning into an exceptionally intense proselyte to the new side. These practices were new to start with and would regularly be upheld relying upon who was in control. After some time, the term of mental programming was created and some more methods were acquainted all together with make the training increasingly all inclusive.

The fresher procedures would depend on the field of brain science since a large number of those thoughts were utilized to show how individuals may alter their perspectives. There are numerous means that accompany the mentally conditioning procedure. It isn't something that is going to simply transpire when you stroll down the road and converse with somebody that you have quite recently met.

For one thing, one of the principal necessities that accompany mentally conditioning being fruitful is that the subject must be kept in confinement. On the off chance that the subject can be around other individuals and impacts, they will figure out how to think as an individual and the mental conditioning won't be successful by any stretch of the imagination. When the subject is in confinement, they will experience a procedure that is intended to separate their own self.

They are informed that every one of the things they know are false and is made to have a craving for all that they do isn't right. Following quite a while of experiencing the majority of this, the subject will feel like they are awful and the blame will overpower them. When they have achieved this point, the specialist will begin to lead them towards the new conviction framework and personality that is wanted.

The subject will be persuaded that the new decisions are on the whole their very own thus it is bound to stick. The entire procedure of mental programming can take numerous months to even years. It isn't something that will occur in only a discussion and generally it won't most likely occur outside of jail camps and a couple of separated cases. Part 2 will broadly expound of what happens during the three primary phases of mentally programming and how the entire procedure happens.

Generally, the individuals who experience mentally programming have done as such when somebody is simply attempting to induce them of another perspective. For instance, on the off chance that you are in contention with a companion and they persuade you that their thoughts bode well, you have in fact experienced mentally programming. Of course, it probably won't be shrewd and you had the option to consider everything sensibly, except you were as yet persuaded to change the convictions that you held previously.

It is uncommon that somebody experiences genuine mentally conditioning where they will have their entire worth framework supplanted. It will, as a rule, happen during the way toward coming around to another perspective, paying little mind to whether the strategies utilized were coercive or not.

Real Life Cases of Brainwashing

Brainwashing as court defense.

All through history, people claim that they committed heinous atrocities because they were brainwashed. This excuse many adopted in the hope of saving their own lives or getting away with mass killings or some other crime against humanity. It might be something as simple as theft. Whichever was the action, brainwashing became an easy defense because it removed the action's responsibility from the accused and it was a hard task to ascertain whether someone was brainwashed or not.

The use of brainwashing pleas as a defense in a court of law is debatable. Most professionals believe that by allowing this defense in a courtroom, the courts would be swarmed with false claims of brainwashing and the means of proving or disproving this defense would be beyond what the courts can handle. However, there have been various cases brought to the courts which showed the validity of brainwashing as a defense for crimes committed.

One such case occurred in 1979. Patty Hearst, who was the heiress to an enormous publishing fortune, used brainwashing as a defense when she faced trial for a bank robbery. Back in 1974, Patty was abducted by the Symbionese Liberation Army (SLA) and ended up joining the group. At trial, Patty reported that she was locked up in a closet for some days after her abduction. During her stay in the closet, Patty stated that she had fears for her life and safety, was brutalized and was starved of food while her captors kept feeding her with their ideologies against a capitalist country. Within two months of her abduction, Patty had changed her name and also released a statement saying that her family was 'pig-Hearst.' She later appeared on the security tape of a bank she was robbing along with her abductors.

Patty Hearst stood trial for this bank theft in 1976 and F. Lee Bailey defended her. It was claimed in the defense that the SLA had brainwashed Hearst. Hearst had been forced to commit a crime that she would never have committed under any other circumstance due to this brainwashing. She did not have the ability to differentiate between what was right and what was wrong under the mental state that she was, due to the brainwashing and therefore, could not be found guilty of the robbery at the bank. The court found her guilty instead and did not agree with this analysis. She was put in prison for 7 years. President Carter commuted her sentence just a couple of years after, so she ended up spending only 2 years altogether in prison.

Lee Boyd Malvo Case

The Lee Boyd Malvo case is another popular brainwashing defense. This case made use of the defense of brainwashed-to-insanity, and the case ended up in the courtrooms around 30 years after that of Patty Hearst. Lee Boyd Malvo was on trial in 2002 for his role in the sniper attacks that happened around and in Washington D.C. During the killing spree, Malvo, who was 17 years of age then, with John Allen Muhammad, 42 years of age, killed 10 people in total and wounded 3. For this case, the defense used was that Muhammad had brainwashed the young Malvo to commit the crimes. The defense made claims that the crimes would not have been committed by Malvo if he had not been under Muhammad's control, just like in the Hearst case.

Malvo's mother had abandoned him when he was a boy of 15 years on the Antigua Island in the Caribbean as indicated by the background story the defense used. In 2001, Muhammad met the kid and brought him into the United States. At that time, Muhammad was an army veteran and worked to fill the teen's head with visions of an approaching race war. With that in mind, Malvo had training to be an expert marksman. Muhammad put Malvo in isolation from other individuals while being saturated with the acrid and eccentric Islam brand that Muhammad followed along with a strict routine of exercise and diet. This is in addition to sharing these ideas with him. The majority of this is believed to have contributed to the brainwashing process on the young teen.

The defense argued that Malvo had been brainwashed by Muhammad because of the time spent with him, and due to this, he was not capable of differentiating what was appropriate from what was wrong. Malvo was pronounced guilty and he was sentenced to life imprisonment with no chance of parole despite the defense's efforts. Muhammad was sentenced to the death penalty in a different trial.

Up until this point, it does not appear that brainwashing will gain much ground as a type of defense in the courtroom. To begin with, proving that a defendant has been brainwashed is very difficult. Next, it is really unlikely that an individual has undergone brainwashing and the defense is simply making use of it as a way to get a lighter sentence or to get their client's actions forgiven instead. Additionally, numerous juries seem to find the brainwashing idea totally ridiculous. Generally, this defense will most likely not see a great deal of strength growing in courtrooms.

Chapter 4: Application of hypnosis

Hypnosis as an art, a field of study or as an idea, has been in existence for a long time. Hence, it has been applied to various aspects of life for good. Its various applications cut across many fields of human endeavors such as self-improvement, military, entertainment, and the medical field. New areas where hypnosis is being applied are physical therapy, sports, rehabilitation, education, and forensic investigations. These days, artists are using hypnotism as a way of attaining certain creative purposes. An individual who has applied hypnotism among other techniques for person creative purpose is the surrealist Andre Breton. Among the new and rising field where hypnosis is being applied in the area of self-development; most individuals have tried self-hypnosis as a way of losing some weight, quitting a bad habit such as smoking, getting over a bad experience and reducing stress.

Various applications of hypnosis, as well as new fields of application, are discussed below:

Applications in the Military

Apart from helping individuals battling with various health issues and addictions, various efforts have been made to apply hypnosis to the military field as well. The American military have made an attempt in this regard. According to a top secret but later declassified document that was retrieved through the Freedom of Information Act stores recently, it was proved clearly that the act of hypnosis had already been researched in the military. Sadly, the report from the research showed that there really wasn't any proof that the process of hypnosis would be applicable to the military field. Also, there was no evidence that showed vividly that hypnosis really exists as a real phenomenon aside the subject of high motivation, expectancy, and mere suggestion.

The document explains how it would be difficult if not almost impossible for hypnosis to be applied in the military world. It states:

"The application of hypnosis in intelligence would lead to certain technical challenges that are not encountered in the hospital or medical laboratory. For instance, if you want to obtain compliance from a resistant subject, it would be imperative to hypnotize the subject under certain important hostile conditions. However, there are no good clinical nor experimental evidence that proves that this is possible."

The report from the classified document further explained the difficulty faced when the researchers attempted to study the outcome and possible application of hypnotism in the military. This is because no-one has been able to state with utmost certainty if hypnosis is a unique state with some specific responses or simply a type of suggestion that is produced because of the positive association between the hypnotist and subject.

Hypnosis as a form of therapy (Hypnotherapy)

Hypnotherapy is a form of psychotherapy using the process of hypnosis. This form of therapy is used to help subjects battling with various issues bothering their minds, especially in cases where other forms of therapy such as self-control have proved abortive. Certified psychologists and doctors may try out a form of hypnotherapy on voluntary subjects in a bid to assist the subjects deal with anxiety, post-traumatic stress, insomnia, bulimia, compulsive gambling, and depression.

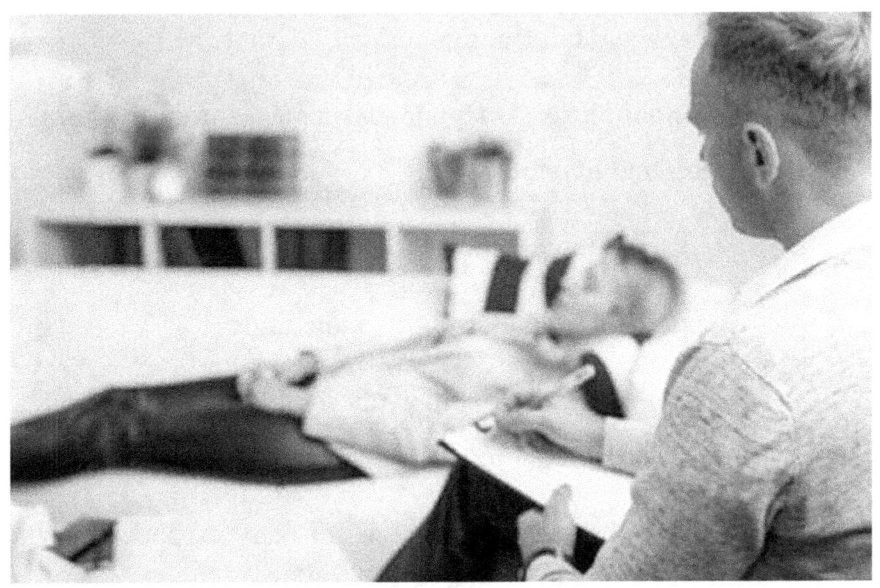

An individual can decide to book a session with a certified hypnotherapist to assist in managing an issue such as help in quitting smoking. It is important to keep in mind that a certified hypnotherapist is neither a psychologist nor a doctor, so they will simply be able to help you get hypnotized but not with a cure to serious illnesses. Therefore, be sure that your hypnotherapist is certified to provide you with these services. Whether to choose a hypnotherapist or a physician is totally up to you.

In modern history, there are various forms of hypnotherapy. Each with a different level of success and depends on the challenges faced by the subject(s). These various forms include:

- **Cognitive-behavioral hypnotherapy** - This is a combination of various elements, cognitive-behavioral therapy and clinical hypnosis;

- **Hypnoanalysis** – Hypnoanalysis is a modern form of regression hypnotherapy;

- Ericksonian hypnotherapy;

- Hypnotherapy to assist with addictions;

- Hypnotherapy can help with soothing patients who are anxious before undergoing surgery;

- Reduce feelings of nausea in cancer patients while treating them with chemotherapy;

- Managing pain during dental care;

- Treating skin diseases such as psoriasis and warts;

- Reducing symptoms of Irritable Bowel Syndrome;

- Hypnotherapy to help athletes improve their performance in a competition;

- Hypnotherapy to help with weight loss;

- Managing chronic pain such as rheumatoid arthritis;

- Managing and alleviating pain associated with childbirth;

- Hypnotherapy can help in dealing with skin diseases;

- Hypnosis to help with management of fears (phobias);

- Hypnotherapy to help with behavioral control;

- Hypnotherapy to help with pain management, especially those suffering from chronic pain;

- Hypnotherapy to can also help with psychological therapy which the patient is battling with;

- Hypnotherapy to aid with relaxation.;

- Minimizing the symptoms observed in those having dementia.

The above are just a few areas where hypnosis can be applied. Although, most people believe that hypnosis can be used as a tool to manipulate a subject and induce them to do horrible things acts or renounce their own faith, all these are mere misconceptions. The most common application of hypnosis is directed towards improving the health of the subject (therapy).

Self-hypnosis

There are some situations in which a qualified hypnotherapist or another expert are not available, and an individual may choose to hypnotize himself. This process can be carried out by using auto-suggestion strategy. The main application of this method is for self-development and most individuals will attempt it in a bid to minimize their stress levels, stop smoking, or to improve their diet. Some individuals find it easy to self-hypnotize, most individuals need some help with getting hypnotized. Such help could include mind machine devices or hypnotic recordings to help them get hypnotized. Other aspects where self-hypnosis is applicable include help in relaxing, to get overcome fear of crowd and with physical well-being.

Stage Hypnosis

Whenever people hear of hypnosis, what comes to mind is stage hypnosis which is a form of entertainment that usually takes place in a club or a theatre in front of a crowd. The performer (hypnotist) is considered as a spectacular showman and this enhances the concept that hypnosis is entirely about manipulation of the mind. At the start of the show, the performer will try to put the entire crowd under an altered state before choosing an individual who fits the criteria to come on the podium and to be subjected to various embarrassing performances under the watch of the crowd.

The reason why stage hypnosis is so effective is still a mystery, though it is widely believed that there is a combination of physical manipulation, stagecraft, trickery, suggestibility, participant selection, and psychological factors. Mainly, experts think that the volunteer is simply conforming to the biddings of the hypnotist and providing a form of entertainment. These volunteers may want to do this because they wish to draw attention to themselves, the desire to satisfy others, and the fear of making it easy to get the volunteer to perform. Some books that were written by some stage hypnotists supports the concept of deception, trickery and some are absolutely made up of false hypnosis where secret whispers were used all through the performance.

Chapter 5: Seduction using dark psychology

Seduction and sexual conquest are sometimes common features of dark psychology. In fact, they will show up so often that we are going to devote this chapter to them and how they work. This is an important topic to discuss because all of us have been, or know someone who has been seduced by someone else who used these dark psychological principles.

The human sex drive can be a very powerful urge and not being able to fulfill it can sometimes lead to unhappiness, worry, and stress in the person's life. On the other side of things, some of the most famous historical figures are known for their frequent and full fulfillment of sexual urges. For example, emperors and kings have often been afforded the finest women as their reward just because of their status.

One example that is very famous is the powerful seducer King Henry the 8 from England. His appetite for women was so strong that he decided to create a new religion in his country so that he could change his wife and marry any woman that he chose. He also exercised utter control over all the wives he had, and many of them were beheaded when they didn't satisfy his needs or help him meet his goals any longer.

This begs the question: Is all seduction a form of dark psychological seduction? Of course not! Yes, all seduction is going to involve the perusal of the other person. Those who don't have the skills of dark manipulation will do this in a clumsy manner. This is shown in some of the popular romantic comedies that come out, where the clumsy guy keeps making mistakes when they try to pursue the girl.

But a dark seducer is going to be someone who knows what they want and they know how to get it. They will go after the other person in order to fulfill their own personal needs, and often they don't really care how the other person feels about it. They can be charming and they are not going to be clumsy at all, and they always know the right thing to say and do.

Why Do People Choose Dark Psychological Seduction?

One question that people will have is: Why would someone want to choose this path for attraction? Is it not a better idea to go on some dates and court someone in an honest manner?

A dark seducer doesn't really want to get into a relationship, at least not into the boring stuff with it. They want to just get certain things out of the area of romance. They don't really care about the other person because they know they can use the techniques of dark psychology to find another partner later on if this one goes south later on. This allows them to approach life, and the relationship, with a non-needy and carefree mindset. If the seducer does decide to settle down with someone later on, they are going to be able to do it without feeling like they rushed or settled into the first relationship to get what they want.

So, how is a dark seducer have so much success and influence within the world of dating? It is because they understand the dark psychology principles and they have the right skills in order to execute these principles.

One of the key advantages that the users of dark psychology will have over their rivals, especially in the world of dating, is that they understand the human mind, almost like a secret weapon. While others may feel like the human mind is impossible to understand, the dark seducer is able to read it like a book and get the information that they want from it.

Someone who works on the principles behind dark psychology in the dating world may find that it is really going to change their dating experiences when compared to their past efforts. They will have a feeling of confidence and control, rather than feeling doubtful, needy, and insecure.

Sure, it may seem kind of mean. The dark seducer is able to jump from one partner to another, using each one in the manner that matters most to the seducer. And there are people who are harmed in this process, especially the ones who are looking for more of a long-term relationship, or those who are looking for more out of it.

But a dark seducer is only interested in what matters to them and nothing else. They can read the mind of their victim and be the exact person that victim wants. But they only do this to get their foot in the door and get what they want. As soon as the victim isn't meeting the needs of the seducer, then the seducer will move on.

Where Does Dark Seduction Begin?

Now that we have an idea of the basics of dark seduction, it is time to move into some of the steps of how this seduction can work. Most dark seducers are going to have a guiding approach that is going to motivate their efforts. They will also have tactics that are going to come from their philosophy. Let's take a look at some of the different philosophies that are there that a dark seducer may choose to use.

One approach is the deployment of a process that is rigid and structured. These seducers feel that they have mapped out how the sequence of attraction should be in great detail and they may have a process that seems like it is from a flowchart. They want their seduction process to be replicable and predictable. These systems not only work for the dark seducer but can work for others who understand these systems and learn how to implement them in the proper manner.

These seducers are going to use a series of stages in their process. They will try to get the target to go through a range of emotions. This range is designed by the seducer to fit their own needs. They will move them through emotions such as interest, attraction, and then excitement. These seducers will see the whole process as a series of checkpoints that they need to pass through to help them reach their goals.

The strength of this method is that it gives the dark seducer a feeling of certainty because they know the exact steps to take each time. They won't have any surprises that come up during the seduction, and it kind of becomes routine and habitual for the seducer. The biggest problem with this is that it doesn't take into account that sometimes people are going to be unpredictable and won't go along with the structured emotional program that the seducer planned out.

Another option is the natural approach. This approach is going to involve the dark seducer cultivating a genuine emotional state internal to the seducer and then expressing them freely to the one they are working to seduce. An example of this is when a person who uses this is likely to spend some time trying to understand their own emotions and then try to perfect these. They are then going to express these to others. The philosophy behind this one is that "I can't make others feel good until I can feel good."

You can also work with hypnotic and Neuro-Linguistic Programming (NLP) seduction. NLP is a combination of neurological processes, language, and behavior. This is kind of a subset of dark seduction. Unlike the structured seduction that we talked about before or even the natural version, NLP and hypnotic seduction are going to involve triggering specific emotional states in the victim and then linking these back to the seducer.

Let's look at an example of this. The NLP approach to seduction is going to involve allowing a person to explore their own intense positive emotions. The seducer may even try to get more of those emotions out. Then, they will work to anchor these to the seducer. That way, when the victim sees the seducer, they will naturally feel an intense physical pleasure, even though they may not know why that happens.

Hypnotic seduction is another option to work with, but it can be a difficult one to work with on a regular basis. This is because few things are going to make someone suspicious about a seducer than the odd techniques that come with NLP. The other seduction types are going to seem somewhat normal to the victim, but hypnotic seduction doesn't seem this way. However, there are some who will respond to it.

Dark seduction can allow the seducer the ability to get exactly what they want out of the relationship. It can sometimes be used by those who are not looking to take advantage of others, but who are open about what they are doing and just use the techniques to give them more confidence and avoid a boring relationship. But there are plenty of dark seducers who use it as a way to use the other person, with no care about how it is going to affect the other person at all. Either way, it is still important to be on the lookout for this kind of behavior so that you don't end up getting into a relationship that is bad for you or isn't what you are looking for from the other person.

Chapter 6: The history of persuasion

Persuasion is another type of mind control that will be talked about. While there probably won't be as much media publicity about this type of mind control as there is with mentally conditioning and hypnosis, it very well may be similarly as successful whenever done effectively.

The issue with this structure is that there are simply such a large number of various types of persuasion that are available in everyday life that it tends to be hard for any one source to break through to the subject and have any kind of effect. While influence attempts to change the considerations and the convictions of the subject like different types of mind control, it appears as though everybody is attempting to convince you about something so it winds up simpler to disregard the influence that is coming towards the subject.

For instance, the plugs on TV, when contention is going on, or notwithstanding when a discussion is going on there is some type of influence that is happening. Individuals will regularly utilize influence to further their potential benefit without taking note. This section will go into more insights regarding influence and how it very well may be viably utilized as a type of mind control.

What is Persuasion?

To begin with, is the meaning of persuasion? At the point when individuals consider persuasion, they will regularly think of various answers.

Some may think about the ads and publicizing that they see surrounding them that desire the buy of a specific item over another. Others may consider persuasion in the terms of legislative issues and how the hopefuls may attempt to influence the voters' assessment so as to get another vote. Both of these are instances of influence on the grounds that the message is attempting to change how the subject is thinking. Persuasion can be found in everyday life and it's a ground-breaking power just as significant impact regarding the matter and society.

Promoting, broad communications, lawful choices, and governmental issues all will be impacted by how influence functions and thusly it will take a shot at inducing the subject too. As can be seen, there are some key contrasts among influence and different types of mind control which have been talked about so far in this manual. Mentally programming and mesmerizing will require the subject to be in disconnection so as to alter their perspectives and personality. Control will likewise take a shot at only one individual to get to the last objective.

While persuasion should be possible on only one subject to alter their perspective, it is likewise conceivable to utilize influence on a bigger scale so as to induce an entire gathering or even society to change how they are thinking. This can make it considerably increasingly compelling, and maybe perilous, on the grounds that it can change the psyches of numerous individuals at the same time as opposed to the brain of only a solitary subject. Numerous individuals fall under the bogus impression that they are safe with the impacts of influence.

They feel that they would most likely observe any attempt to seal the deal that i tossed their direction, regardless of whether the specialist is really selling an item or some new thought, and afterward have the option to grasp the circumstance that is Going on and discover the end through their own rationale.

In certain situations this will be valid; nobody succumbs to all that they hear the majority of when they use rationale, particularly in the event that it goes totally against their convictions, regardless of how solid the contention might be.

Also, most subjects will probably stay away from the messages about acquiring TVs and extravagant autos or the freshest item available. Ordinarily, the demonstration of influence will be substantially more unpretentious and it tends to be increasingly hard for the subject to shape their very own sentiments about what they are being told.

At the point when the demonstration of influence is raised, a great many people are going to see it in an antagonistic light. They will think about a sales rep or a conman who is attempting to persuade them to change the majority of their convictions and who is going to push and trouble them until the change happens.

While this absolutely is one approach to consider influence, this procedure can frequently be utilized in a positive manner as opposed to only a negative way. For instance, open administration crusades can urge individuals to stop smoking or reuse can be types of influence that can improve the lives of the subject. It is all in how the procedure of influence is utilized.

Components of Persuasion

Likewise, with different types of mind control, there are sure components to be kept an eye out for with regards to persuasion. These components help to characterize precisely what influence is with the goal that it is increasingly conspicuous.

As indicated by Perloff in 2003, influence is characterized as "A representative procedure where interchanges attempt to persuade other individuals to change their frames of mind or practices with respect to an issue through the transmission of a message in an environment of free decision."

This is something that makes influence unique in relation to different types of mind control; the subject is frequently permitted to settle on their own free decisions in the issue regardless of whether the strategies of influence are getting down to business to move the subject's psyche in a specific course. The subject can pick what direction they need to think, in the event that they need to buy an item or not, or on the off chance that they think the proof behind the influence is sufficiently able to alter their perspectives.

There are a couple of components that are available in influence that help to characterize it much further. These components include:

- Persuasion is representative which implies that it uses sounds, pictures, and words to get the point over.

- Persuasion will include the operator intentionally endeavoring to impact the subject or gathering.

- Self-influence is a key piece of this procedure. The subject is typically not forced and rather they are given the opportunity to pick their own choice.

- There are numerous ways that influential messages can be transmitted including eye to eye, web, radio, and TV. The correspondence can likewise happen nonverbally or verbally.

How about we take a gander at every one of these focuses in somewhat more detail. The primary component of influence is that it should be representative. So as to convince somebody to think or act with a specific goal in mind, you should most likely demonstrate to them why they should change their contemplations.

This will incorporate the utilization of words, sounds, and pictures to get the new point over. You can go through words to begin a discussion or contention to demonstrate your point. Pictures are an incredible method to demonstrate the proof that is expected to influence somebody to go one way or the other. Some nonverbal prompts are conceivable, yet they are not going to be as powerful as utilizing the words and pictures.

The subsequent key is that influence will be utilized in a purposeful manner so as to impact the manner in which others are acting or thinking. This one is entirely self-evident, in the event that you are not deliberately attempting to impact others, you are not utilizing influence to get them to change. The persuader is going to attempt various strategies so as to get the subject to think a similar way that they do.

This could be something as straightforward as simply having a discussion with them or exhibiting proof that supports their perspective. Then again, it could get significantly more included and incorporate increasingly beguiling structures to alter the subject's perspective. Progressively about the strategies that are utilized in influence will be examined later in this section.

The one of a kind thing about influence is that it enables the subject to have some type of choice. The subject is permitted to settle on their own decision in the way. Generally, regardless of how hard somebody attempts to convince them of something, they don't need to pull out all the stops. The subject may tune in to a thousand plugs about the best vehicle to buy, yet in the event that they don't care for that brand or are not needing another vehicle around then, they are not going to go out and buy it.

On the off chance that the subject is against fetus removal, it won't make any difference what number of individuals turn out and state how incredible premature birth is, the subject isn't probably going to alter their perspective. This permits significantly more opportunity of decision than what is found in different types of mind control, which may clarify why numerous individuals don't consider this to be a sort of mind control when inquired.

Persuasion is a type of mind control that can happen from various perspectives. While mentally conditioning, spellbinding, and control need to happen on an up close and personal premise, and now and again in complete seclusion, influence is fit for happening in different ways. You can discover instances of influence everywhere including when you are conversing with individuals you know, on the Web, and through radio and TV. It is likewise conceivable to give powerful messages through nonverbal and verbal methods; in spite of the fact that it is significantly more compelling when verbal systems are utilized.

Chapter 7: How to recognize the art of manipulation

It's interesting to see that manipulation has been around for a long time, and that is not a new or imaginary concept. Understanding what the art of persuasion is really all about is vital, to help you to deal with it.

In this chapter, we will look briefly at the psychology of manipulation. This allows us to see where it might occur in our lives. It will also help you in identifying those who might attempt to manipulate you. It is not only about people who like to dominate. If we don't know it is happening to us, might be encouraged to act in ways that are incongruous to our normal personality and behavior. Learn how commerce can persuade customers into buying their goods and services. Recognizing such methods will help in dealing with the power of persuasion.

We like to believe that we are individuals who make sensible choices. In our personal journey of life, we do not always have full control, and we don't always realize this. As children, we are influenced by our parents and have little control over how we raised. Once in the education system, we are further manipulated. The teachers will tell us all about the social norms and what is expected of us in society. As adults, we are lured in by politicians trying to get their share of votes. Many are persuaded to vote for a party because of what they promise for the future, even if they don't necessarily believe in their policies. This gives such politicians power, and their decisions will affect our lives. Are we really in control of our lives, or are we merely influenced by those who know all the tricks of persuasion?

Later in this book, we will look at how to deal with various manipulative methods, even sometimes covert. First, you need to learn to recognize when you are being manipulated so you can counteract it. For this purpose, we will now look at what the experts say on how this sort of behavior can exist among us.

Are you feeling manipulated?

What then, in our everyday lives, do we need to be wary of?

<u>Persuasive Language</u>

The idiom that every picture tells a story, is very true. Words can be so much more powerful as they inspire and encourage us, even to the point of manipulation. How many times have you been inspired by a good orator, whose daring speech motives you into action? Words even influence when we are lost completely in a great book. The art of words can be so influential in coercing us to believe something, even when our eyes tell us differently. Communication is a powerful tool, especially when it comes to making people do things.

Six Theories on Psychological Manipulation

<u>1 Cognitive</u>

There are many well recognized psychological processes in theories regarding the art of persuasion. One of those is the Cognitive Response model, developed by Anthony Greenwald in 1968. It is still relevant today for determining some factors in persuasion. It is also a model used extensively in the world of advertising.

Greenwald suggested that:

It is not the words of the message that determines the success of persuasion, but more the emotions of the **receiver**. The internal monologue of the one receiving the message will be deciding factor on how easy they are influenced. Such internal thoughts will include positive and negative aspects, according to the individual's own personality. This not a learning process, but more based on whether the person already views the message with favorable or unfavorable thought processes (cognitions).

Overcoming any counter-arguments will rely on the expertise of the **persuader**. They should stop their target from having sufficient time to construct any counter-arguments. The **persuader** must encourage positive arguments to come to the forefront. This gives the "persuasion effect" a better chance of success.

Persuasion can be more difficult if the intended target has been forewarned. It allows the target time to build their own counter-arguments, if the "message" is counter-intuitive to their present cognitions. The importance in pre-warning can be seen in research conducted by Richard E. Petty, in 1977. The study showed that students given notice about a certain event were less likely to be persuaded that those who had no pre-warning.

2 Reciprocity

Another well-studied explanation for how we might be open to the power of persuasion is the Rule of Reciprocity. This is based on a principle related to social conventions. If someone does you a favor, or does something good for you, then you are more likely to feel obliged to return the favor.

The Rule of Reciprocity can also happen subconsciously. Without even realizing it, you may agree to an action or favor asked of you by the requester. All because at some point they had done something for you, and you feel in their debt. You may feel obliged even if the request is something you would normally decline.

It is an effect widely used by companies who are looking to make sales. Often companies give out free samples, or time-limited trials. This is not without a motive. It is in the hope that the customer feels obliged to return the favor, and buy the product or continue with the agreement.

Reciprocity is a recognized psychological process. It is an adaptive behavior which would have increased our chances of survival in the past. By helping others, it is likely that at some later point they will help you. Though, it can also have negative effects. If someone does something bad to you, then you may be driven by the rules of reciprocity to exact your revenge.

The Rule of Reciprocity is well supported by academic research. Burger et al (2009), suggested that a group of participants were more likely to agree to a request if the requester had previously done them a favor.

3 Information Manipulation

A powerful tool in the manipulator's armory. This is a method of being outright deceitful. It is a means of providing limited and confusing information to the victim. The effect of this will unbalance their way of thinking, making them vulnerable. It can also incorporate the use of intentional body language, to persuade and manipulate someone.

A study by McCornack et al. (1992) showed the different ways a message can be falsified to assist in the manipulation process. McCornack's theory has a premise of four maxims, in a truthful statement. A breach of any of these will render the message as intentionally deceitful. The four maxims are:

Quantity

This is the "amount" of information provided. Most of us seek to provide the right amount of information so that the receiver understands our message. Not too little, or too much, as that might confuse. A manipulator though would play with that quantity of information. They may omit certain pieces they consider irrelevant.

Most especially if it is likely to work against their argument. This is known as "lying by omission."

Quality

Refers to the "accuracy" of the information provided. Truthful communication is one of High Quality. If we were to violate this maxim, then the receiver hears intentional mistruths. This is "outright lying," to gain the manipulator power.

Relation

Here, we talk about the "relevance" of the information to the message. To confuse or sidestep an awkward question, the manipulator may go off topic. This is a way of changing the subject, for the sole purpose of misleading. It could be to hide their own weaknesses. Or even to over-emphasize on something that will give them more power over their listener.

Manner

The "presentation" of the message. An important aspect of this is body language. We read inflections and facial expressions as we listen. A manipulator may exaggerate these to mislead the presentation of the message. This is all in the aim to emphasize their own agenda.

Lying to manipulate or persuade someone is not a new concept. It is though, a method that is becoming particularly potent in the modern world. Online communication and social media do not always involve face-to-face contact. This makes it easier to tell mistruths or exaggerate information. A manipulator may in their elements with such communications.

4 Nudge

Not all manipulation is sinister. Sometimes we may be manipulated to help us make the right decisions for our own good. To do this, the Nudge Theory is particularly useful. The Nudge Theory expands positive reinforcement, by using small nudges.

Skinner's studies or behaviorism, show how useful this theory can be. With positive reinforcement, such as rewards, it can manipulate people into behaving in the manner that you are hoping to encourage.

One example of "nudging" can be seen in this example. Adding exceptionally high priced items on a menu may seem counterproductive. Yet, the result of this actually increased the sales of the second highest priced item. The customers were given a "nudge" in the right direction, but for the benefit of the restauranteur.

Richard Thaler, considered the father of the Nudge Theory, was awarded the Nobel Memorial Prize in Economic Sciences. His contribution to behavioral economics was considered quite momentous. Nudge Theory gives positive reinforcement, or as Thaler described it, it gives "nudges."

The Nudge Theory is not only effective in economics. It can be used to encourage behavioral changes and influencing personal choices.

Even accepted social norms can be manipulated to changes, in this way.

Nudging is so successful, that in 2010, the British Government set up a Department Behavioral Insights Team. This was to help develop policies. The department was referred to as the Nudge Unit.

There can be obvious benefits of using "nudges" to influence people. It is still a form of psychological manipulation that can infringe on an individual's civil liberties.

5. Social Manipulation

This type of manipulation is also known as psychological manipulation. It is often a tool for politicians, or other groups of powerful people who are used to advancing their own interests. In its worst form, it is a means of social control. By taking away individuality, it coerces the populace into accepting what is given to them. Though it can have a positive side when used to help with personal issues, such as improving health and wellbeing.

Those in power who use social manipulation may use distractive techniques to deflect from important issues. They would argue that their proposals are for the benefit of the populace, and the benefit of your family and its future. Anything you think personally, that might be different, is wrong and selfish. This type of persuasion is very paternalistic, almost treating individuals as if they were all children. This "system" will strive to make the crowds believe the things that have gone wrong are, in fact, their own fault. The only way to resolve the problem is to listen to the guidance of those who know better.

Such a political strategy would bring to forefront one social problem, only to hide another. It is a tactic to cause social unrest and panic among the populace. By creating unease in society, the populace will begin to demand changes. An example could be that the department wishes to hide the problems health care. So, they decrease the budget in crime prevention, causing crime statistics to rocket. The populace will receive information to coerce them into believing the best way forward for the crime problem. The politicians will feed propaganda, by disseminating their own **truths and facts**. It may not always be true, or it may be information that is exaggerated, such as misuse of statistics. This type of social manipulation could take years to get the end result that the manipulator requires.

The use of psychological manipulation is all a part of social influence. Professor Preston Ni, Communication Studies, published an article in Psychology Today. He indicates that **one party recognizes another's weaknesses. They deliberately set out to cause an imbalance of power. This enables them to exploit their victims, for their own agenda.**

Does this make us all social puppets? To some degree, it does. Most of us comply and conform to what is expected of us to avoid a society of chaos.

Think for a moment, what is the latest gadget or home improvement product that you would like to buy? Is it something a friend told you about, or a neighbor owns? Chances are it is something that someone else has, or you've read that it's popular on the internet, and that makes you desire it. This is another side of social manipulation. We can be so easily swayed if we let our guard down. Whether that is a good or bad thing, depends on how you personally view it.

As mentioned earlier, not all social manipulation is a bad thing. it can have positive aspects. The word "manipulation" might conjure up thoughts of a villainous individual/s bending you to their will. But, used correctly, social manipulation can help the populace, as a whole. Good examples of social manipulation are the "5 a day campaigns." Health specialists attempt to convince us to eat more fruit and vegetables. Or even the "stop smoking campaigns," which have resulted in reduced numbers of smokers. The result of which is a reduction in smoking-related diseases. This is coercion at its best.

6 Gaslighting

This is perhaps the cruelest form of manipulation. It is a means of casting into doubt on the sanity and self-esteem of a person. You could say it is **sowing the seeds of doubt** into the victim of manipulation. Working on a similar principle such as "knowing you are being told repeated lies." Until eventually you begin to believe the lies as the truth.

It is an unkind form of manipulation. The **gas-lighter** will cause their victim to lose all confidence in their own credibility. This leads to completely destroying their own self-worth. All because they begin to doubt themselves. That is the intention of **gaslighting**, to reduce the victim to a psychological mess. The manipulator will constantly put their target down by contradicting them. Also by convincing them that they are always wrong. Sometimes to the point that the victim will be accused of telling lies. This is why the victim loses all self-esteem. When that happens, they become ruled by the domineering influencer. It is a form of mental abuse, often seen in abusive personal relationships. The influencer will use constant techniques to make their victim doubt themselves. Even to the point of doubting their own memories, by denying things they've said and done.

Gaslighting takes a while before it is fully effective. The manipulator will wear his/her victim down over a long period of time. This type of manipulation is so insidious that it can eventually lead to the victim doubting their own sanity.

Dr. George Simon PhD is a Clinical Psychologist at a Texas university. He has studied people with disturbing personalities. The results of his studies caused him to believe that certain types of personalities, particularly psychopaths, are very adept at manipulation. They will distort the truth and use aggressive language, to set the wheels of doubt in motion in their victim's thoughts. Eventually, the target will lose confidence in their own judgment. They may feel shame and they will come to believe that the manipulator is right. This puts the target under the manipulator's control.

Gaslighting is not only restricted to individuals acting on one other. It can be argued that it also has political uses. Columnist and author Maureen Dowd is one to follow this belief. She argued that Clinton's administration used gas lighting techniques against a political opponent. Newt Gingrich, a member of the opposing political party, was often goaded into appearing hysterical. Some journalists and psychologists argue that Donald Trump also used gas-lighting techniques. Not only during his presidential campaign but also whilst in office. They argue he frequently says one thing, then denies he ever said it, which is classic gas-lighting.

Your partner is manipulating you

Let's look at some examples of how manipulation manifests itself in personal relationships. Perhaps you can see some of these traits in yours?

- Manipulators are always control-freaks. The more control they have, the more they sink their teeth into the victim.

- They will violate other people's personal boundaries. It could come in the form of snooping and spying, or even more bold open actions. To enable them to do this, you will be allowed nothing personal, such as your phone or computer. They will pry your passwords from you, in some sly way. At the same time, they jealously guard their own boundaries, being the first to complain if their personal space is breached.

- They may force your hand, such as stopping you from seeing your own friends. They do not want to share what is theirs, and you are their property. To start with they will show you that they don't like your friends. Inside, they see them as a threat. Jealousy is taken to the extreme and may even become aggressive.

- If you make a decision without them, they will not be happy. They don't want you to have free will, otherwise one day that decision may be to leave them!

- Their control may appear in the form of advice, though you have little or no choice but to accept it. They are not advising you, they are instructing you in what to do, and how to behave.

- It is not unusual, in fact, it is usually essential that a manipulative partner will want to know your daily routine. Step out of that routine, and they will interrogate you for it.

- You may notice that they often criticize anything you say, particularly in public. Belittling your opinions and thoughts gives them a sense of, "they know best." Another means of imposing their power over you.

- Not only do they enjoy putting you down, but they may go the extra mile. Accusing you of lying or having a bad memory, or even having the cheek to call you the manipulator.

- You can never please a controlling manipulator. If you think you have got to that point, they move their own goal posts. This is a relationship whereby you never know exactly where you stand.

If you are in a manipulative and abusive relationship, then no doubt it will be an unhappy one. Manipulators can be very unpredictable. Often, they turn to rage at what they see as a violation of their rules.

It is not easy to break out of such a relationship, but there are some agencies that can help. When you can do this safely, search the web for local organizations that assist victims of abusive partners. Don't forget to delete your browsing history because nothing is private from a manipulator. The stress in on your own safety, but you must seek that help. Our last chapter will give you more guidance on how to build up courage, because the chances are that you are now a quivering wreck.

Your friends are manipulating you

Is it always easy to make friends in a new environment? Of course not! Sometimes it is extremely intimidating and at other times, downright hostile. Other times, you feel like fish out of water. Everybody needs friends and learning how to attract them is an important life skill we should all have. Human beings are fundamentally social animals who seek out the company of others and there are very few exceptions to that rule.

Choosing friends – Drawing the kind of friends you'd like to have

Here are three broad categories of friends:

Hello-Bye-bye friends (acquaintances)

These are people who become your friends almost automatically, by virtue of finding yourselves in the same environment, like your workplace, for example. You say "hello" when you meet the first time in the day and you say "bye-bye" as you wind up for the day. Once away from the shared environment, these friends (which are actually only acquaintances) rarely have any further involvement with you. They're nice to know and they can be valuable allies, due to their skills, but they're not necessarily the sort of people you can count on one hand. (The Greeks say that you can count true friends on one hand – that's something to keep in mind).

The Average Buddy

Drinking buddies, golf buddies, shopping pals – fun time friends come and go. They share with you the things about life that make it fun, because they're fun. They like to laugh and enjoy your company. The lighter side of life is where these friends are going to pop up. These aren't necessarily people you engage in long conversations about the meaning of life, or the reality of climate change. This is your loose social circle, developed over time, that enjoys a good time as much as you do. They come and go and when you meet, a good time is had by all, but there's little in the way of depth in the relationship.

Soul friends

These are the 3:00 am phone call friends. You know they'll be ready to talk if you wake them from a sound sleep. These are the people you can go on a road trip with and not want to kill before you've even hit Route 66.

Long, probing conversations, shared secrets and mutual support are what these friends are all about. People who stick with you, through thick and thin, are soul friends. They're the people who have an intimate understanding of what makes you tick and you return the favor. Some of these friends may be with you from childhood until death. Others, you may pick up along the way. What distinguishes them from the hello bye-byes and average buddies is the depth of the relationship. You may go years without seeing a soul friend, but when you finally meet up again, it's as though no time has passed. You pick up where you left off, because you know each other so well and you were meant to be friends. These are the ones who are the hardest to find and also the ones you long for. Soul friends are a reflection of who we are and what we really care about. Even more than that, they're the people we know we can always count on, because they know exactly who we are.

Forming genuine friendships takes time

True friends are not made overnight. True, lasting and intimate friendships evolve over time, due to a genuine chemistry that exists between the people involved. Like romantic relationships, friendships are based in a fundamental chemical exchange which speaks to both parties like a song. You know when it's real. You can't create these bonds. They're pre-existing realities that you can only recognize and act on. When true friends; soul friends come into your life, the impact will be unforgettable. You will know immediately that the person you've just met is intended to be with you (in whatever capacity) until the end of your life. Soul friends may not always be at our side, physically, but they will always be at our side, spiritually. Where ever we are and whatever we're doing, we know they're there. We know we can pick up the phone, call and find them ready to talk to us. These are the friends who are with us until we're no longer living and breathing. That's what makes them so special and so incredibly important.

While we may recognize a soul friend at first sight, the world is not a place in which bonds are easily formed on this level. Soul friends, despite the distrust we've all learned to live with in the modern world, will look beyond that initial reticence and continue showing up. They won't give up. They'll seek you out, even when they don't know they're doing it and you'll do the same. Over time, the bond will become unbreakable and you will have made a friend for life.

Here is how you can become adept at making new friends:

Don't over think

Have you been apprehensive about meeting someone only for you to feel at home with them in the first two minutes of meeting? The fact is that if you are meeting a person for the first time, you have no idea how they are or how they behave. Why bother analyzing everything half to death?

And again, assuming that meeting with a new person is bound to be scary only serves to make you fearful of the moment. The fear then makes you wary of the meeting; sometimes even making you detest it. In fact, for the most part, the reason you find yourself feeling somewhat shy towards a person is because of the fear you are harboring of having an encounter with them, or anyone else for that matter. Life makes us into individual silos of isolation. It makes us suspicious. Bad experiences with other people can stunt our ability to form the kind of bonds we're actually hungry for – the kind of bonds that last a life time. The best solution, therefore, is to disabuse yourself of the notion that meeting people you are not familiar with is scary. Stop over-thinking about how to carry out that first conversation; how to connect with people who are actually the kind of people you need in your life. Overthinking the forging of the most important connections in our lives can make of us sad, isolated people who never really connect with others in the profound and lasting way that human beings were intended to connect.

After all, who is to tell if the other party is not anxious about meeting you? We're all anxious in these latter days. We're all suspicious and nervous and continually asking ourselves if the people we meet have the right motivations; if they're genuine. Most of us are thinking the same thing. We've lost our trust in one another.

So relax and create in your mind a positive image of that first encounter; a healthy image. In any case, there are plenty of people out there who may judge you unfairly on your first encounter. Everyone carries around a collection of cultural assumptions about the composition of people who are worth knowing. You have them too. The trick is to open yourself to others and to allow the universe to connect you. It works very well, if you'll allow it to happen. People worth having as friends know better than to judge a person on superficial grounds. In summary, fear is in your mind – get rid of it! Let go of your accumulated fears and presuppositions and, instead, rely on your intuitive powers and your newly-established ability to read people. You know enough to understand when people are honest or not. You've learned to read their mannerisms, their speech patterns, their facial expressions and other non-verbal indicators about who they are. Trust yourself and your knowledge. You're more than ready to sift the wheat from the chaff, which means there's absolutely nothing to fear; no cause for suspicion or reticence.

You're now more than ready to throw yourself out into the social whirl and find the kind of people who deserve to have as friends. With your new skills, rooted in the practice of social psychology, you're going to be able to establish rather quickly who is naughty and who is nice. The Big Bad Wolf is out there, but you're not Little Red Riding Hood anymore. You're now a proficient and capable, socially aware person. No one's pulling the wool over your eyes anymore. With your new knowledge, it will be easy for you to discern, from the people you meet, who is going to be the kind of friend you need in your life. There's no more guesswork, because you know the ropes now.

Move at your own pace

If you have been out of the social scene for a while, you may feel overwhelmed meeting new people, as you ease yourself back into it (say in a seminar or even a party). However, you can pre-empt that problem by seeking out individual friends or acquaintances who you expect to be in attendance. You can meet with them before the event and catch up. This will put you more at ease with throwing yourself back into the social whirl. By the time you get to the event you won't feel as anxious. For one, you'll know people who are going to be there. They can introduce you to other people. For another, your friends will be aware that you're anxious. They'll shepherd you. Never be shy about reaching out to people you know for support. As we've learned in the course of this book – that's what friends are for.

Just in case you are you're seeking to move back into having a social life again, after having been a little sequestered, here are some great ways to ease yourself back in:

- Begin by reaching out to acquaintances – the hello-bye bye category is a good place to start. There's not a lot to lose here.

- Extend your social circle to include small groups of people you are friends with, just to observe the dynamics of people relating; familiarizing yourself with being around groups of people again. It doesn't have to be scary. You can ease yourself back in.

- Expand your social circle by accompanying your friends when they are meeting with others. Make it known that you're hoping to move back into a more active social life. Most people will be happy to help you do that.

- Break out of your comfort zone and begin accepting invitations to mix with people, even those not in your close circle of friends. They say that you can't get to the sweetest fruit without going out on a limb, so climb out there. Learn to relish the opportunity to have new experiences with new people. You're learning more about yourself now and about other people. Why not get out there and put some of that knowledge into practice? After all, why shouldn't people want to meet someone as interesting and intelligent as you are?

Be pro-active in socializing

Once you you've become re-acquainted with the practice of seeking out new social connections and when you are no longer in your solitary cocoon, you can begin to pro-actively seek out people you know and others who are new to you. You can begin branching out from the foundation that your friends and acquaintances have provided by moving further into the social milieu, into areas that may be a little unfamiliar. For example:

- Join a group or groups whose members share your hobbies and other interests.

- Enroll to participate in workshops or to pursue courses of study which interest you. It's quite easy to make friends in a group in which all the members share a common interest.

- Volunteer and you'll be happy to serve as you make new friends in the process. While you're at it, you'll develop skills and aptitudes you may have hoped to make more viable. In the same way as workshops or groups, the common core of interest will provide a jumping off point for bonding with others volunteering with you.

- Accept invitations to birthday parties, various celebrations, and other social functions. You never know who'll meet at gatherings like these. Break through you own barriers. These may be preventing the type of people you want to connect with from connecting with you.

- Be open to attending social events and even "meet ups", based on common interests. It also doesn't hurt to go out to the bar every now and again. There are people sitting in bars in every city of the world, just looking for someone interesting to talk to. Maybe, just like you, they're looking for a way out of isolation, or social stagnation. Your horizons expand when you demand that they do. No one is going to push them outward for you.

- Join online communities – while these may be located in cyberspace, but I know personally that they can result in real world friendships. I've made many real world friends on Facebook and other online communities. Sometimes, it's easier to share your thoughts in writing, than it is in spoken conversation. This is just one more avenue for making the kind of lasting connections you're hoping to. BONUS: You get to analyze the written communication style of potential new friends before you actually meet them!

Take the initiative

There's no reason you should wait for others to approach you. They're just as reserved as you are, after all. Nobody is born knowing anyone else unless they're family and even then, it's a bit of a crapshoot. You can approach people to start a conversation, by employing simple questions, like "how are you" and "where are you from". It's not hard and you've absolutely nothing to lose. Be open to the people around you and you'll be surprised at how readily they'll respond to that openness.

Remember you are trying to break the ice between you and a stranger, so avoid over-talking. Be warm, but not overly insistent and don't get discouraged if others don't respond immediately. Always try to put yourself in the place of the other person. Employ the lessons you've learned in this book to figure out where they stand and try to meet them there. Be gentle in your judgments of others, though, remembering always that we all judge one another. Take the time to let the person you're engaging revealing themselves to you, just as they're hoping you'll reveal yourself to them.

Fight any temptation to be judgmental

No one's perfect and that includes you. We tend to evaluate people quite harshly before we get to know them. This is a function of our survival instinct, which tells us that the fewer people we allow near us, the less potential there is for danger. But we're modern people and we can do better than that. Besides, you now have in your command a variety of skills concerning non-verbal language that can help you sift through the people who very obviously aren't the sort of folks you're looking for.

Remaining open to those we meet is the door to better friendships and more of them. Not writing people off because of petty complaints about the way they look, or speak, or dress is the best way we can become more flexible about who we welcome as friends and that's the real secret. Sometimes, it's the most unlikely person who is going to prove to be our very best and long-term friend. Everyone is looking for the kind of friends we believe we deserve, but we should always ask ourselves if we meet our own qualifications. You may find that, in asking yourself this question honestly, you discover shortcomings in yourself you might not be willing to tolerate in other people. As I've said repeatedly in this book, knowing yourself is the key to knowing other people, so don't overlook amending your own challenges before you start writing other people off as potential friends, due to their own.

Chapter 8: Tips how to deal with manipulative people

Manipulative people can seem to be everywhere. Most manipulation is not necessarily oppressive. Not every stranger asking you to do something is a controlling manipulative person.

Everyone can be a little manipulative when they need to be, so not every manipulative person is bad.

Take your time to identify a person whom you suspect to be a control freak. Do they come across as selfish? Are they approachable? Do they seem excessively bossy?

1 Ground rules.

What you have read so far will help you to identify the difference between persuasion and manipulation. Persuasion may be for yours or the teams own benefit, manipulation is always for the controller's benefit. Examples could be: is what you are being asked to do within your normal remit? Are they asking you to rush something through for the team, or for their own personal remit? Will this benefit you, or make you look bad? Do you like and trust this person?

There are ways you can deal with a manipulator, should you have the misfortune to meet one.

2 Observe a manipulator before you label them.

It is not unusual in a workplace to have people telling you what to do. So long as they ask in the correct manner and they have the authority. Authority comes in many guises. It could be because they are your managers, or they are close work colleagues. If the request is genuine, then it should not be a problem. If someone is constantly demanding you to do things with aggressive coercion, then you are right to be suspicious. Don't jump the gun though, take your time. You don't want to overreact and ruin a workplace relationship unnecessarily.

Observe their behavior whenever you can, without them realizing what you are doing. Keep your distance because you don't want to attract this character's attention. It is important to identify this person for what they are, so you to keep them at a distance in the future.

How then do you handle them when you have to be in their presence?

3 Never let them see your own weaknesses.

If you recognize someone to be a controlling manipulative person, it might be best that you have as little contact with them as possible. This can be difficult in a working environment, but try to restrict personal contact with them. That way, you are not likely to ever divulge your personal life or any problems you may be having. The last thing you want is for them to recognize any of your own weaknesses. They may use that information to gain a hold over you.

Example: You accidentally ate someone else's yogurt in the kitchen area, at work. It was a genuine mistake, you thought it was yours. The owner of the yogurt kicks up a fuss about who has "stolen" their yogurt. You want to admit it, but you keep your head down and stay quiet. Unfortunately for you, the manipulative person saw you eating the yogurt. The likelihood is that they will not give you away, but instead store the information away. At some point in the future, they will tell you that they kept your secret. This is an innocuous example, but it shows how easy it is to become ensnared by a manipulative individual. It is from such humble beginnings that an expert manipulator is able to get under your skin. Once in their clutches, it can be hard to break away.

The best option is to be open and honest. If you can handle your own weaknesses, then how can a control freak find a hold on you?

4 Never allow them to put you down, especially in front of others.

A common psychological phenomenon often exploited by manipulator's is Imposter syndrome. This is a phenomenon that has been well studied. At least 70% of people will suffer from Imposter syndrome at some time in their life (6a). It includes that dreaded feeling of inadequacy at whatever you attempt to do. Even if there is evidence that shows you otherwise, such as your own success at your work. You feel a fraud and you are simply waiting for someone to announce it. That someone may very well be the office manipulator. Except, of course, they are not uncovering you because you are perfectly proficient at your job. What they are actually doing is working on your own feelings of inadequacy. It's how manipulators work, especially the more invasive ones.

When you stand up to a manipulator, they can become abusive. A forceful manipulator will not let people stand in the way of their primary objective. Everyone is fair game in their attempts at power-play. If there is one in your work environment, it will only be a matter of time before they turn their attention to you.

What can you do?

- Show them your confident side, especially if this person is constantly putting people down. You know them for what they are.

- Convince yourself that anything they say is untrue.

- Do not allow them to break you, and do not bend to their will. Try not to be confrontational with them, that could make matters worse, but stand up for yourself.

- Sometimes, the best strategy is to take it on the chin, and walk away. If their schemes and plans do not affect you, they will soon lose interest.

- Don't bluster in front of them, that is a sign of weakness.

- Show your strengths and the attitude that you have no care about what they think or say.

- Then pat yourself on the back and walk away.

- It is important that any conversation you have with them is never on a personal level. They may try to make it personal but you must steer them away.

If someone does not treat you with respect, then show your contempt in a respectful way. Then, turn your back on them.

If someone is making unreasonable demands of you, stay clear of them whenever you can. If you can't meet their needs and they complain, be brave. Explain the truth of the situation but not in a defensive manner. Try not to be hostile or confrontational in any way, but don't allow them to walk all over you.

If you are successful at rebutting their attempts to manipulate you, they may become aggressive and personal. Now they may attempt the Imposter syndrome. This is where the insults of incompetent, inadequate and useless may come at you. Keep your calm and keep a distance of space between you. Don't apologize, that's what they want you to do. Trust in your own instincts and advise them to go to your supervisor with their complaints. If they are your supervisor, then let them know that you may need to take this further up the ladder of management. If you say this with commitment, they may falter. If you say it with fear, it may be time to walk away and indicate that you will speak with them once they calm down.

If the situation gets to this point, you may want to find someone you can trust to help you calm down. Tell them what happened so you can get it off your own chest. It was a disturbing situation, but you must be able to move on from it. Don't brood and don't be fearful of them.

They may not calm down and start making you a target of their abuse. Now is the time to be looking at making that complaint to those in a higher authority. Before you do that, begin to document your evidence of any future events involving you both. This will provide you with evidence for the day you decide to go ahead and report them. Whether your boss will accept your complaint is irrelevant. You have evidence to back up your argument and it could be enough for the manipulator to back off. Sadly, they will only find someone else to pick on unless the senior management accepts that there is a problem.

If you are regularly under the spell of a narcissistic manipulator, then will have low self-esteem. You MUST build up your self-confidence and become more powerful within yourself. Only then will you be able to break the chains they have wrapped around you.

5 How to leave a control freak

For many people, especially women, this can happen in the family home. For such victims, trying to break free is the most difficult. Not the least because the victim may, in fact, love their toxic partner or parent. If you are in such an unhappy situation then you must consider your own wellbeing and safety. Only if the perpetrator can admit that they have a problem and seek help, can they begin to mend. If they learn to compromise and accept your input, then it will be a great step forward. Such an openness may save a two-way partnership. The problem is though, such a manipulator cannot see that they are making your life a misery. If they are so blind, how can they ever accept that something is wrong? Indeed, if you approach them they may become defensive and aggressive. This is because they perceive you as having insulted their integrity and pride. How dare you accuse them of anything!

Unfortunately, if you are in such a relationship then the only way you will be free is to make the break yourself. The adage, **"You only have this one life, live it to the fullest,"** is never apter than in this situation.

How though, do you find the courage to leave? That is exactly what it will take to be rid of such an overpowering partner. They may even continue to threaten you after you have dared to leave. That is one of the reasons why you dare not make that move.

How then do you build up your confidence to finally leave the relationship?

6 Begin with building up a support network.

It is vital that you have support from friends and family. This can be a difficult one though. It could be that the very partner you have just left, browbeat you to severing all personal ties. If this is your situation and you are unable to pick up those ties, then there are organizations that you can turn to. These agencies can guide you on dealing with your situation.

It is going to be a rough ride and you may even need a safe house where your partner does not know where to find you. Don't feel ashamed. If you have children it will be even harder, but for their sakes, get them away. They can make contact again in later years if they so wish. Then they may better understand what happened. Bear this in mind that if you feel stifled, then almost certainly they do too.

That is, of course, the worst scenario. No matter how hard it is for you to leave, you must take the time for yourself, and recoup.

7 Don't forget your own health needs.

Do things that help you relax, if possible. Get outside and take short walks. You need personal space so you can consider your situation. Listening to music you like or immersing yourself in a book or a TV program, is good if it helps you to switch off. Avoid overeating or drinking too much alcohol. Your problem will become tenfold if you take that route. All these points are double stressed if you have children. You need to stay strong for them, and for yourself.

8 Accept that you will feel scared.

If your partner has sensed anything, they could revert to being overly nice to you. Don't be fooled, you know without anyone having to tell you that it will not last. It will only be natural to hesitate in your actions, whether it is out of fondness, pity, or fear. Fear of being on your own is natural. Fear of your partner's violence is not. If that's something you feel, then you are most certainly making the right choice. If you do leave, then you must make it quick and clean, leaving no trace of where you are going. Manipulative, obsessive partners will attempt to track down fleeing partners, even if only to punish them. You have broken their self-ego and now they have no one left to control. If they do find you, they may try the extra-nice approach and beg you to return, or they may be violent and angry. You don't want to be there for any confrontations whatsoever.

If possible, then make a complete break and move to a new city. I know this might not seem practical and a little extreme, but you do want to bump into such an ex-partner. Most cities and large communities have agencies to help victims of domestic violence, to start afresh. It won't be easy but it will be worth it. Consider all your options before you put your plan in motion, because you may need to be tucked away for a while.

9 What are the after stages?

Once you make the break, accept that it is permanent. This one chance may be the only opportunity you get. Everyone's motives and decisions for making such a daring move are individual choices. It can be especially difficult if children are involved. Often, those who have managed to make the break can eventually give in. It could be out of a sense of pity, or a false sense of being beholden. The controlling partner will offer to change their ways, and could even manage to do it, but most do not. You may give in thinking they cannot live without you around to help them. This is a form of pity and you should fight it off. If you give in, you will go right back to square one. Be selfish and think about yourself for a change. Perhaps you might feel lonely and that in retrospect life together wasn't that bad. This is a natural reaction at first, but tell yourself, if it had not been that bad, why did you leave?

Remember that your own confidence will still be at a low level, even if you managed to leave the abusive relationship. It is going to take time to heal, as any injury does. Get to know your own self once again. You have lost touch with your own needs and what you desired out of life before your relationship. You need time so you can build up your own self-esteem and find out what you want out of your new life. It may take years before you recover, so be patient with yourself.

You may lack the courage to face a world that suddenly seems huge and overwhelming. Compounding that is the fact that you might not even have yourself a home, once you leave. That should be your priority, searching for a place you can call home, somewhere you will feel safe. Finding employment, or schools for the children can follow. These can all be remedied in time, so don't expect all the answers immediately.

Eventually, you will begin to trust yourself and believe in your own decisions. Make sure you do things that you enjoy, even if it is only reading a book. Your mind needs to adjust to this strange independence you have gained. You may even feel lost without having someone to make all the decisions for you. Allow yourself time, that is all it takes.

Don't worry if you don't make friends very easy; you have been out of the loop for a long time. Anyway, you need to pick and choose your new friendships carefully. The last thing you want is to meet another domineering personality. It may result in a few trust issues on your part, but that is not important. You have every right to be cautious.

<u>10 Build up your courage.</u>

Once you have built up your courage and self-esteem, you can then face the world head-on. We all approach this one in a different way. The first rule must be, not to compare yourself to others. It is not an easy rule to follow, but nonetheless, you are new to freedom. That is exactly what you are, free. Forget other people. Of course, be polite, but concentrate on your needs and not anyone else's, unless you have children.

There will come a time when you must begin to take risks. That is after the huge risk you have put yourself through by leaving. You have taken a huge leap forward, no need to jump in feet first, give it time to settle.

A great exercise for those who are worriers, is to write down all the worst situations you feel may befall you. Once you have a thorough list, the next stage is to consider how you might deal with each of them. Take notes on your best plan and strategy. This will show you the problem from a detached perspective. It will help you determine which approach is best for each situation. If you feel it is too overwhelming, then break it down into smaller and more manageable steps. As you tackle each micro-step, before you know it, you will have reached the last one. Baby steps do lead to resolving the whole of the problem.

You will make mistakes! the proverb, "to err is human," is true. You need to embrace any mistakes you make and learn by them Learning the right way to do something is so much easier when you have knowledge of the wrong way. You're not perfect, no one is, but you only need to be as perfect as you yourself want to be.

Chapter 9: How your dark side works

Your dark side does not understand good intentions, it does not compromise, and it does not want you to do what you want it to do. Although it is suppressed, it is growing and looking for opportunities to surface. What many people are ignorant of is that it is important to fathom this dark side within us and regain control of ourselves, to understand each other and to get to know each other.

What does the dark side feed on in you?

The dark side of your mind feeds on personal suffering and self-destructive behavior, everything that you reject, and all those desires that just do not seem to come true.

Your unmet needs create in you negative emotions that the dark side can consume in you. If you fail to meet these needs, then those negative feelings will cause something bad to grow inside you. And they will make you believe that this is even your true self or maybe even the only self-hidden within you.

There are many things that you know you should not do because you realize that they are bad for you and yet you do them. You are well aware that it would be better not to smoke, that you should not constantly eat greasy food, that you should not always yell at your partner or your children, that you do not always get involved in infertile discussions let that ultimately lead you nowhere ... but these things happen to you anyway.

For the dark side in you are not just good intentions. Either you pick up the booklet and stop offering it a breeding ground, or it will continue to gain room in you.

How to get what you want

What does your dark side need?

To stop nurturing your dark side, you need to become aware of the things you most want. It's about negative psychological dependencies those feelings that make you focus on a certain state with all you might, causing pain in you.

These negative dependencies keep you from feeling safe, in good shape, and strong. And they find expression in rejection, humiliation, deceit and the feeling of being useless or failing.

All these negative things keep the darker sides in your soul alive. They grow in parallel with your negative feelings, thoughts, and actions and are also supported by toxic persons you have or had in your life.

Every time something negative happens in your life, and every time you remember something you do not like, that dark side of yourself that is connected with that negative attitude and its right to a place in you comes to the fore seems to throb. Then it seems that there is no way out, and in this way, you only attract more personal suffering, self-destruction, and negativity, which in turn provides you with a new breeding ground.

How can you confront the negative side in you?

It is possible to confront the negative side of your mind through conscious training. Some things cannot be eliminated that way. But those who can do that should be confronted, and you should become aware of them. The biggest challenge is to explore your inner self and shed light on what is hidden deep in you.

The dark side of us can hide much better than an unfulfilled wish, a frustrated hope, or a broken dream. But you are the only person who can immerse yourself in you and explore you closely.

And every time that something negative comes up in your life, every time you feel like something sinister in you trying to grab the helm, you have to try to get to the bottom of it without being ashamed of it have to.

First of all, you have to accept that there is a negative side in you and that it will not disappear just because you are trying to suppress it. Trying to suppress her will only make her stronger, and with this new strength, she would simply explode as soon as she gets the chance.

Meditation can help in this process. A mentor can also help. Art, too, can be a way to tackle the worst things in your mind and let the entire negative out of you.

Only when you start to do the things that the dark side is trying to hide within you will you be able to regain control of your life and learn to handle the negative, so that it will no longer be in control has about you.

Males Of The Dark Triad: Why Women Are Attracted To Bad Guys

The attraction of the "bad guys," the hard guys with internal problems is well known: they suffer from it, and they consider it very unfair.

The attraction of the "bad guys," the men with conflicting personalities, the hard guys with internal problems are well known: they suffer it, and they declare it unfair ("why do you always become friends with those who treat you well and Do you like imbeciles? ").

The paradox is well known and, although you can have intuitions about it, the causes of this attraction have never been exactly ruled out. However, a previous study by the University of Durham, led by Gregory Louis Carter, brings a new vision about this phenomenon.

The masculine traits

Research has revealed that many more men than women possess what in psychology is known as the dark triad, which consists of having remarkable personality traits based on narcissism, psychopathy, and Machiavellianism. This includes a dominant attitude and a grandiosely distorted conception of oneself.

Studies show, then, that in the case of men, narcissism is overwhelmingly greater, without distinction between some cultures and others. Also, it is believed that this narcissism is related to the short-term mating that occurs in men since it is related to "the will and ability to compete with one's sex and to repel couples immediately after the sexual relationship." Along the equivalent lines, and according to the authors of the study, narcissists tend to start new relationships, again and again, identifying all the mating options. They are, thus, less monogamous.

Psychopathy, on the other hand, tends to be a guarantee of insensibility and lack of empathy, as well as a marked antisocial behavior. It also tends to success in short-term relationships, because it supposes a great moral deficit and a great hostility in personal relationships. Also, psychopaths tend to show a false, superficial charm and a social attitude that tends towards sexual exploitation.

Machiavellianism is linked to duplicity, lack of sincerity, and extroversion. These individuals exercise opportunistic manipulation and coercion, advantageous, like the previous characteristics, in short-term mating. Studies reveal that Machiavellian men are by the system, more promiscuous.

The investigations that had been carried out to date established that men who present the dark triad have much more sexual success than others. However, as Carter mentions, many of these studies have been based on data provided by the participants themselves: that is, men who present the dark triad are described as more sexually successful than others. That is why, having investigated only one point of view, Carter wondered what the vision of women would be, and why they found a certain appeal in the dark triad.

The feminine opinion

To get something clear about such issues, Carter's team gathered 128, who were introduced to a man who owned the dark triad or did not own it. After the presentation, the participants answered a series of questions on a scale of one to six about the attractiveness of the personality of the individual in question. Also, some factors that influence the attraction, such as the level of education or wealth, were omitted ex profeso.

The researchers' conclusions were clear: women found greater attractiveness in men who had the dark triad. The result reinforces previous studies, in which these men perceived themselves as more sexually attractive.

The Explanation Of The Attractiveness Of Conflicting Types

The Carter team offers two explanations for this phenomenon. Consider, first of all, that sexual selection may have something to do with it. This would imply that women are responding to the signs of "male quality" in terms of reproduction. And about short-term relationships, this would translate into the attraction that women experience towards "bad guys," who show security, stubbornness, and recklessness.

Second, sexual conflict is also at stake. Researchers say that "women may be responding to the ability of men to sell themselves." Men with dark triad are very effective manipulators and captivators. In any case, we must recall that the fact that women found this type of men more attractive does not mean that they were chosen to be the father of their children.

Chapter 10: How to manipulate people

Manipulation is nothing but a technique that can be used to influencer person to serve a positive or negative intent. Eminent social psychologist Robert B. Cialdini listed six influence principles that when mastered allow you to pretty much influence people and influencer their thoughts and behavior.

1. Reciprocity – People almost always have a compelling urge to return other's favors. "Oh! She bought me a really expensive gift. I must do something for her too." Do not these words seem all too familiar? If you really wish to get someone to do something for you in future, start by making them obliged to you. Keep reinforcing verbally the things that have been doing for them as a favor. For example, say something like "Oh! You'd do the same for me, or you'd help me too, wouldn't you?" instead of saying, "not a problem at all or do not mention it please." You are simply trying to tell them that you expect them to help out or do something you want them to in future.

2. Social Proof – Good or bad, people are more often than not hardwired to follow the herd since man's primitive hunting and gathering days. People automatically assume that just because everyone else is doing it, it must be good or right. This is precisely how trends, fads, and fashions take off. Presenting social proof allows you to influence people because it leads them to believe that they aren't the only ones doing something. Do not you ask the host upon being invited to party about who all will be attending it? Aren't you likelier to go when you realize that almost everyone from your social circle will be there? You do not want to be left out, do you?

3. Scarcity – It is human tendency to value things that we believe are rarely available or limited. Think about how carefully business owners and marketers influence consumers with their often false "limited sales," "last few products remaining," "exclusive offer only available to selected customers" "until stocks last" etc. There is a tendency to grab what is viewed or perceived as scarce.

4. Liking - Be honest when you answer this. There is an attractive looking and pleasant talking in store A that is the exact same thing that is being sold by a plain looking and not so confident salesperson in store B. As a customer, who are you likely to buy from even though both seem like really good people? We are more influenced by affable, charismatic and physically attractive people. Similarly spending plenty of time with a person is a great way to get them to be familiar with you or like you. Want to ask your crush out on a date? Spend lots of time just hanging out with them as friends before taking the plunge. They will be less likely to refuse because you're now familiar and hence liked by them.

5. Commitment and Consistency - When you get people to commit to something, it's easier to influence them to fulfill it. For instance, if you get someone to make a public declaration about something or get them to commit to it in writing, there will higher chances of them following it for fear of being held accountable for it later. When you really want someone to do something, get them to commit to it in writing or say it where others can clearly hear them say it. This way, they can't really backtrack or risk being seen as someone who does not fulfill what they commit to.

6. Authority – Why do you think all those health and hygiene product advertisements and promotional videos have "experts" talking about how people will benefit from using these products? Ever wondered by social media influencers are highly paid to promote a product, service or idea on their social media channels? Because people lap up authority. Anyone who holds a certain position of authority, power or expertise in a given domain is highly regarded by people. If you truly want to influence people or get them to do what you want them to, introduce a person who perceived to be in a position of authority to say what you want them to do.

Again, whether you use these techniques in a negative way to achieve a devious objective or harness it positively for influencing people and bringing about a constructive change is totally up to you. Remember you're holding a powerful matchstick in your hand that can either light up a flame or cause a disastrous fire.

Convert and take over

After gaining self-awareness and connecting with your true self, you must develop the ability to make sure that everything you have discovered thus far works for your good. This ability is what we contact emotional intelligence self-management.

EQ self-regulation or self-management involves governing your feelings. With self-management, you are able to gain total control over your reactions. The goal with this is to be able to have positive emotions towards all circumstances. Self-management will not totally eliminate your feelings of anger nonetheless it does provide you with the ability to control and learn to convert it into positive energy. You may use this energy to seek solutions to situations that would generally cause anger.

So how exactly carry out you put the feelings you've identified as well as any kind of emotions that may unexpectedly arise under your whole control? It may look like a lot to handle but through the advancement of self-regulation abilities you will find it to become sort of second character. EQ self-management comprises of many facets such as stress administration, intentionality, integrity, achievement travel, emotional self-control, being proactive genuinely, taking positive initiative, and versatility, among numerous others. All these tenets help you realize and cope with potential behavioral complications before they get out of hands and degenerate into devastating consequences.

Developing Emotional Self-control

Before diving into this area of the guide, it is important to learn that both positive and negative emotions can take control over you. Don't be fooled by the positive emotions that seem enjoyable as they envelop you. Normally as they can bring you to new heights just, you could be brought by them crashing down if they're not controlled.

They can lead you astray and make you lie to yourself about particular things since they make you feel great. So, both positive and negative emotions work against you when you allow them to take control. It is therefore essential to master emotions of all kinds so that you can take complete charge of your life; not allowing yourself to react with techniques that are detrimental to yourself and to others.

You can form Emotional self-control through the following steps:

Identify & Validate Your Feelings: That's where your self-awareness practice is necessary. Validating your emotions and being honest about any of it is undoubtedly an extremely critical step in managing it. Now you are aware of your emotions it is necessary to ask, are any of them managing you? Are they worthy of feeling? Can they advantage you if controlled? Do they feel great or bad? When they are linked to the feelings of other folks you may want to talk to why they might be feeling the way they perform and whether you are responding properly or if you are reacting in a manner that is harmful to your emotional stability.

If you notice that people's critical emotions towards you are hurtful, think about ways that these feelings may become good for you (Can they help you build upon emotional control? Grow in some real way you hardly ever thought of before? Etc..). In any case, you cannot defeat an enemy you do not know anything about or haven't even known. By validating any emotions that we or other folks have, we give the emotions a tone of voice and a face, that makes it easy to devise approaches for overcoming them. In providing them with a real face and name, we start noticing the energy that they have over us.

Map Your Triggers:

It is possible to do this in your thoughts but it helps to get yourself a notebook and jot down any state of affairs or events that result in each of the emotions you've identified. After discovering that you have an issue with an emotion like anger, after that you can start 'mapping' the things that result in you to possess anger outbursts. Write down the occasions preceding a certain emotional reaction. Once you are able to do this, breaking your 'automated' reaction to any triggers becomes easier and in change makes it possible to really start controlling your emotions.

Develop a Plan of action: It is necessary to arm yourself since you go out in to the world where any of your triggers may appear at any moment. Devise some positive "self-talk" and keenly listen to it, especially in the wake of different triggers. It can be a single term like "peace" or a question such as for example, "am I in charge?". You must do this in whichever method is most effective for you, anything that you can say to yourself that will remind you to assume control. Our reactions to triggers are exaggerated and biased sometimes. If we were to avoid for a brief moment to challenge our automatic a reaction to triggers, downplaying them or controlling them will be a lot easier. While developing and using the self-talk method, visualize being in charge of your feelings. How does it feel? Do you want to reach such circumstances where you remain composed and focused regardless of the prevailing circumstances? Try to answer these queries and focus on your answers. Continue with this technique daily until your individual conversations become your preferred activities.

Practice Your Abilities in Realtime: It is one thing to prepare and practice by yourself but transferring the abilities you've been working on into scenarios as they take place is another. Anytime you identify useless feelings and reactions, choose to swap them with better types. Exercise your capability to respond consciously to any circumstance. Remember to choose calmness in demanding situations; a break could be taken by you from demanding situations, take deep breaths, do a few physical exercises, or drink some water. Certainly, you can't usually leave these situations to go workout or grab water but keep your options open - be adaptable and perform whatever will relax you. This will give you a chance to evaluate your following plan of action and make a decision that's in tandem together with your values.

Reflect: Perform some self-reflection every morning, mid-day and evening (although anytime is okay) and note down what it is you feel that day time. This doesn't require a full meditation - ask questions like, "why do Personally i think sad/unhappy/anxious/angry etc. today?" or "why do I react like this?". As you continue through the entire full day, you will start noticing that you catch yourself reacting to apparently 'innocent' situations inappropriately, that will in turn help you to break the automatic response to different emotional triggers.

Unplug: Encircling yourself with situations that trigger more negativity or psychological outbursts will not help, especially when you are trying to manage your emotions. Instead, you could respond by just steering clear of anything or anyone that triggers non-beneficial emotions for some time. This allows you to regroup and come back stronger and even more with the capacity of responding with level-headedness. You don't necessarily physically need to unplug; you could do that mentally by inducing you to ultimately unplug from such situations or people actually. When you are able to unplug physically, try to spend time alone without distractions (no phone, tv, etc.) and separate yourself from the ties of the exterior world temporarily.

Tip: When managing your feelings, avoid suppressing them unnecessarily. Instead, become increasingly aware of them and make deliberate decisions on how to respond if they resurface. The key point is to identify the underlying factors behind your emotions and engage in positive assessment of your behavior.

Do not be manipulated

We discussed in an earlier chapter how manipulation is a double-edged sword that can be used to fulfill a positive as well as negative purpose. Being a manipulation expert is as much about spotting manipulation and deception in others as it is about leading others to do what you want them to.

Do you want to safeguard yourself from manipulation on a daily basis?

Do you want to prevent people from taking advantage of you for fulfilling their own selfish goals?

Do you want to be able to sniff manipulation from miles away?

Here are brilliant strategies to protect yourself from manipulation.

1. Ignore Their Words and Actions

Manipulators almost always go after shaking people's confidence and making them insecure to get them to do what they (the manipulators) want. They will do their best to plant seeds of apprehension and self-doubt. There is a tendency to make the victim believe that the manipulator's opinion is actually the truth or fact. Rather than wanting to help you, they are more interested in trying to control you.

The best strategy to deal with these negative manipulators is to ignore them rather than trying to argue with them or correct them. This allows them to set an even deeper trap for you. Do not fall for their conflict or confrontation bet. Simply bypass them, without revealing your emotions. Do not let them see the emotions that make you tick. Once they gain a good understanding of your emotional triggers, they will sneakily use it for influencing your thoughts, behavior, and decisions.

Some people are difficult to delete from our life immediately. Think – boss, neighbor, family member, etc. Just pretend to listen to what they are saying, agree with it and eventually do exactly what you want.

2. Trust Your Judgment

Few people know what's good for you as well as you do. You do not have to ask everyone for their opinion and end up coming across as someone who is not sure of himself or herself. You are inviting manipulators into getting you to do what they want if you do not know what you want.

Do not look for definition and validation from other people. Trust your own judgment and feelings. Develop an inner voice that guides you through important decisions in life rather than relying on other people to do for you.

Tune in to your own values, beliefs, strengths, and interests. Hold on to what you believe in strongly. This way you'll be less susceptible to let manipulators make inroads into your thought process and life. Your strong beliefs will prevent them from influencing or affecting you.

3. Do not Compromise

Guilt is one of the most insidious tools used by manipulators to get their victims to do what they want. Of course, it can be used positively to influence a person too, but in negative manipulation, its usage can spell disaster for the victim.

Manipulators induce a feeling of guilt in their victims for their past mistakes, choices, and failures. They will make you guilt about being self-assured and self-confident. Each time you experience happiness, they will make you feel bad about it. Their objective is to never make you feel good about yourself or happy.

They'll sow seeds of self-doubt about your true worth, persona, and abilities. Do not get knocked off balance or feel guilty they start blaming you. Do not doubt your self-worth or abilities. Never believe that you do not deserve happiness or to feel wonderful about yourself. Take pride in who you are and your accomplishments. Build a strong sense of self-esteem and confidence. Do not compromise on your happiness or your feelings about yourself.

4. Do not Fit In, Stand Out

It isn't funny how many people make them susceptible to manipulation by trying hard to fit in. Manipulative people count of your desire to want to fit in to push their agenda. They lead you to believe that everyone does what they want you to do and that those who do not conform are abnormal. That is the only way to control your decisions and behavior.

Give up the notion of trying to fit in, and encourage the idea of standing out among the rest. Be different from other folks. Focus on reinventing yourself, laying your own rules (for what is good for you and others) and avoid cowing down to peer pressure.

5. Stop Seeking Permission

We've been conditioned to ask for permission since childhood, right from when we wanted to be fed as a baby to when we wanted to visit the bathroom in school to waiting for our turn to talk in the boardroom. The result of this conditioning is that people seldom do anything without seeking permission.

There is an excessive focus on being polite and making things comfortable for others. Manipulative people want their victims to live by their own self-drafted, imaginary rules or values. The underlying idea is you are not free to take any decision without consultation. Be brave and give up this sense of confinement. You have the power to change your life without the need to live by someone else's self-fulfilling rules.

6. Do not be a Baby

If you are tricked once, it isn't your fault. However, if you are tricked 15 times, there's something wrong with you. Do not let people take advantage of your by being everyone's favorite punching bag. Have the courage to stand up to manipulators and say a firm no when you know they are taking advantage of you. Stop whining about other people are taking advantage of you, and take complete control of your life.

Victims of manipulation almost always complain about how people use them. No one can take advantage or you without your consent. You are indeed responsible for your own actions and their outcome. If someone has used sneaky tricks to outwit you, it is your fault. Learn from past blunders and stop trusting slippery people again and again. Move away from them. Focus on surrounding yourself with positive, constructive, inspiring and like-minded folks who make you feel good about yourself.

7. Have a Clear Sense of Purpose

When you do not know what you want, you'll be more prone to do whatever everyone else wants. You'll be easily tricked into doing what other people want you to do without a firm goal or objective in life. People who lack a clear purpose or aim tend to function or go through life more mechanically. There is little logic in their actions or decisions. They will be more prone to experiencing a growing sense of emptiness in them that will craftily be filled by a manipulator.

This lack of objective or constructive activities makes the manipulator feel empowered enough to easily distract you or draw you to their agenda.

Have a higher purpose in life. It can be anything from taking up a cause for the betterment of the community to traveling around the world to rising in your professional life. Do not allow manipulators an opportunity to prey on your sense of purposelessness. When you are absolutely clear about where you are headed, it is difficult to stop you or get you to change tracks.

Fear

Much like a manipulator will pick up on weaknesses, they will also zero in on your inner most desires and fears. Many manipulators, well at least you are really experienced and affective ones, will promise you just about anything you could imagine will help you solve the variety of difficulties and struggles that life throws at you. Whether it is the promise to go on a lavish vacation you can't afford on your own or something even more complex, manipulators know how to dangle that carrot in order to reel you in.

The best manipulators will also play on fears the same way they do desires; they offer the promise of protection. Knowing and understanding your fears and desires, plus having a solid handle on the facts that can provide the solutions and help you realize a desire might be out of reach, makes you less of a target for manipulators. The best way to do this is to simply face them head on and honestly evaluate both what you fear and what you truly desire. By acknowledging the worst case scenario for each of your fears, you can make your peace with them and move on without giving these fears any power in your life. Desires need to be mentally catalogued. Those that can be reasonably attained (such as a dream vacation) can be worked for through goal setting. The others should be tucked away and reexamined within a set timeframe. By having a handle on both your fears and desires, you take away any kind of sway anyone could hold over you.

Most of what will help make you a harder target for manipulators is knowing and understanding your weaknesses. Once you have a handle on your weaknesses, you can start to take the necessary steps to effectively deal with them, which can include eliminating them from your life.

While this might sound easy to some of you, for others it might sound like the hardest thing in the world. After all, taking up the proverbial mirror and deeply examining yourself, and thus coming face to face with your weaknesses, is something that many of you have been avoiding for years.

For those of you who are not sure where to start when it comes to taking your personal inventory, there are numerous self-assessment resources available online. These self-assessments can assist you in determining what areas your weaknesses are in. It is important to do this self-assessment right away, because the sooner you know what those weak points or other areas that need improvement are, the sooner you can get started on protecting or improving in those areas, thus reducing your appeal to emotional manipulators.

Emotional Manipulations

If you rely on others' happiness for your own happiness, you are emotionally dependent. Do not fall into the trap of believing that if your spouse or significant other is not happy, then you can't be happy, too. This is a good way to attract emotional manipulators because your behavior is exactly what they want. They want you to be dependent on them for your happiness and joy.

Thus, they can use the carrot stick approach to keep you working for their happiness at the expense of your own. When it comes to some of these traits, they may feed off each other, thus a manipulator can use a variety of tactics to achieve their ends, based on which of your traits is the most dominate at the time.

Therefore, it is important to keep your personal self-worth up to avoid attracting an emotional manipulator. After all, they feed on the traits that a lack of self-worth typically produces. Additionally, below are some more traits that are on the list of manipulators when scouting for their victims.

What Emotional Manipulators Are Looking For

This is a list of the additional traits that emotional manipulators are looking for in their victims. While individuals may struggle with changing these traits, it is still beneficial to take an honest inventory of yourself and work on any potential problem areas. By doing so, you will reduce your risk of attracting these emotional manipulators.

- Dependency: They want someone who will depend on them for emotional support, and eventually financial support. They want you to depend on them for your livelihood because this will ensure you will never want to leave. In this particular case, isolation will be a key tactic of the manipulator, because isolation breeds the dependency the manipulator craves.

- Immaturity: People who are immature are easily manipulated because they are either trying to please or they are trying to get back at a caregiver, and thus will do anything. Again, this falls into the manipulator's plans, because the immature would not question the tactics of the manipulator.

- Naiveté: People who are naïve believe there is no evil in the world and if there is, it won't touch them. A manipulator builds on this worldview, giving the impression that the world is that way, while they are taking from their victim. Thus the naiveté of the victim works against them, because the manipulator is able to shape the world view of their victim to match what the manipulator wants it to be.

- Impressionable: This goes along with immaturity. Those who are impressionable are easily swayed to believe something that is not true. Anyone can use this to alter how someone sees the world, thus turning a victim into some who sees things the way the manipulator wants them to see it. The manipulator's opinions become the victim's and thus the manipulator gains a definite hold on their victim. This makes it even harder to break the hold, because the manipulator is seen as in the right and other who express concern are overreacting. A victim might even isolate themselves from family and loved ones because they believe that those individuals are trying to ruin their relationship with the manipulator.

- Trusting: Someone can be too trusting when it comes to others. They believe that everyone has their best interest in mind and cannot believe that others would do something wrong. For a manipulator, nothing that they are doing is in the long term best interests of their victims. Instead, the victim's trusting nature leaves them vulnerable to the lies and blame game of the manipulator.

- Lonely: Loneliness is a dangerous emotion. It makes humans do anything in order to get rid of it, and that may include allowing a manipulator to come into their life. When someone is looking for companionship, a manipulator sees and individual with few friends that can step in between them and their victims. Loneliness can actually be a lack of a safety net for a potential victim.

- Narcissistic: Manipulators do not always use 'bad' tactics to get what they want. Sometimes they are able to play to people's narcissistic side and flatter them into behaving the way the manipulator wishes. This flattery can be about anything, from clothes to hair and other choices. When an individual falls for the flattery, they often leave the manipulator in the position where they can make the victim think that fulfilling the needs and wants of the manipulator is all their own idea. Yet the reality is that the victim is bring controlled because they aren't willing to take an honest look at their own shortcomings, preferring flattery over self-improvement.

- Impulsive: Those who are impulsive are not in control of their emotions, which makes them a better target. Often they can quickly be turned toward being angry, thus giving the manipulator a chance to use this anger and the actions that accompanied it to build in guilt with their victim. The other way that an impulsive person can be worked on is by encouraging quick decisions without giving the victim time to ask questions or think a matter completely through. As with any tactic or trait, the manipulator is looking for a means to control the thought processes and actions of their victim to achieve their short and long term goals.

- Altruistic: This is the opposite of a psychopath. It's someone who is too honest, too fair, or too empathetic. They always can see how someone else is feeling and they're more easily manipulated by false emotions displayed such as anger and hurt. Remember that almost all manipulators are good actors, feeding on drama whenever it can be used to their advantage. They aren't bound by being fair or honest. After all, one the tactics in a manipulator's arsenal is lying and placing blame whenever possible.

- Masochistic: Masochism is believing that you deserve to be punished for something. This personality trait plays right into the punishment and guilt tactics of a manipulator. They may also continue place fault at the doorstep of their partner, even when their partner is sad or feeling hurt. As the manipulator feeds the feeling of being a bad person, their victim feel as if they serve what happens to them at the hand of the manipulator.

If you display any of these tendencies, you should seek a therapist in order to discuss how to get to the root of the situation better. Often times, there are deeply rooted psychological issues that need to be explored in victims of manipulators. If your examination of your own personality exposes some of these traits before you are a victim of a manipulator, then it is important to learn how to curb them, thus reducing your chances of being caught in a manipulator's web. A psychologist can help with many of these concerns, so don't assume that you can simply fix them for yourself.

Conclusion

People are not as mysterious as they seem and understanding them is not so much a science, as an observational project. Your powers of observation, when it comes to navigating situations at home, with friends and at work, are well within your ability to understand and command. It's all a matter of picking up the clues people liberally offer, as we engage with them.

Now that you understand how Social Psychology applies to your everyday life and how you can use it to improve your business, your career and even your social life, you can start implementing the skills you've learned. You'll be surprised at how fast you'll see positive changes. You'll begin to experience better rapport between you and your co-workers and family, as well as your friends. You'll be more readily able to understand where people are coming from and be less inclined to walk out of any number of incidents and experiences frustrated, asking yourself "What are they thinking?" You now have the tools to accurately read people's emotional and intellectual responses more accurately and that makes you a much more effective and professional person.

This book is a popularization of the amalgam resulting from the melding of sociology and psychology – social psychology. While the two disciplines may still be at odds with one another, when they're reconciled they form a system for interpreting the world around us in very effective and constructive ways. By paying close attention to other people, you'll be able to more confidently move through life. The foundation of that ability is knowing yourself and being in command of the way you present yourself to others. By curating your public presence, you'll be more readily able to discern the undercurrents of other people's psychological and emotional landscapes and to glean important information that will help you live a more successful and peaceful life.

Human beings are complex animals and you're no exception. Knowing your tics and mannerisms is the roadmap to understanding those of others and your ticket to being able to successfully influence them for the good. As I've tried to make clear throughout this book, my goal is to make other people more easily interpretable to you. By detailing some of the primary ways people communicate non-verbally, I hope I've been able to show you how people are much less mysterious than they seem at first glance. Life is a mystery, but people aren't really. People are open books, offering you a wealth of information in the way they present themselves to you. The way they hold themselves, speak, arrange their faces and move their hands. This is all free information which can help you become much more successful at getting a handle on your interactions with others.

You're now able to use the information in this book to be better at everything you do. Every day is a new beginning and every person you meet represents a multitude of possibilities. Every single encounter is a link in the chain of your life. With the knowledge in this book, I'm hoping you'll come to understand how great an opportunity every connection you make is. Everyone you meet, from the bus driver to the CEO of your company, to the spin class instructor, to the barista at your local coffee bar, is an important link in the chain of your life. There's no one person who's going to make a difference to you (although, they're out there and they can be part of it). Your life is a series of encounters that lead to your goals and dreams and each of those encounters is as rich as you make it.

I hope the knowledge you've gained by reading this will lead you forward, and that your journey will be peopled with the kind of intelligent and lively folks that will make it a thrilling tapestry of experience. Sometimes the destination is fun to think about, but if we miss the journey on the way there, we miss out on the best part. Look up from the path, see who's walking with you and then ask yourself – what did they mean by that hand movement? What does that facial expression mean? How do my own mannerisms mirror theirs? You'll figure out what it all means while you're on your way. Just don't forget to enjoy the journey. It really is the very best part.